# Beginning React

G000241176

Greg Lim

# Table of Contents

# PREFACE

## About this book

Developed by Facebook, React is one of the leading frameworks to build efficient web user interfaces. You use small manageable components to build large-scale, data-driven websites without page reloads. No more wasting time hunting for DOM nodes!

In this book, we take you on a fun, hands-on and pragmatic journey to master React from a web development point of view. You'll start building React apps within minutes. Every section is written in a bite-sized manner and straight to the point as I don't want to waste your time (and most certainly mine) on the content you don't need. In the end, you will have what it takes to develop a real-life app.

## Requirements

Basic familiarity with HTML, CSS, Javascript and object-oriented programming

## Contact and Code Examples

The source codes used in this book can be found in my GitHub repository at https://github.com/greglim81.

If you have any comments or questions concerning this book to support@i-ducate.com.

# CHAPTER 1: INTRODUCTION

## 1.1 What is React?

React is a framework released by Facebook for creating Single Page Applications (SPA). What is a Single Page Application? Most web applications are traditionally server-side applications. The server holds the business logic, stores data, and renders the website to the client. When a client clicks on a link, it sends a request to the server, and the server will handle this request and send back a response with html code which the browser will render and be viewed by the user.

The problem here is that with this approach, the server receives a lot of requests. For example, when we go to a website and click on its *Home* page, we send a request for which the server has to respond. We click on the *About* page and it sends another request, and the server responds. We click on *Blog* and it sends another request and again the server responds. Essentially, traditional websites consist of independent HTML pages and when a user navigates these pages, the browser will request and load different HTML documents.

The many requests, response incurs a lot of time and resources spent on these tasks lead to a slow feeling of web pages, whereas the apps on your mobile phone or desktop feel very fast most of the time. React wants to bring this app like feeling to the browser where we don't always have to load new pages each time there is an action from the user.

A user still clicks on various links in a SPA. However, this time, the client handles the requests on its own and will re-render the html page through Javascript, so the server is left out here if no data from the server is needed. This is much faster as we don't have to send data over the Internet. The client doesn't have to wait for the response, and the server doesn't have to render the response.

Also, in a SPA, the browser loads one HTML document and when users navigate through the site, they stay on the same page as Javascript unloads and loads different views of the app onto the same page itself. The user gets a feel that she is navigating through pages but is actually on the same HTML page. Facebook newsfeed is a good example. Other examples are Instagram or Twitter where the content gets dynamically refreshed without requiring you to refresh or navigate to a different page.

*Manipulating DOM Elements Efficiently*

Loading and unloading different views of the same page involve querying and manipulating DOM elements. Such DOM operations involve adding children, removing subtrees and can be really slow. This is where React addresses this shortcoming in manipulating DOM elements efficiently. React does this by updating the browser DOM for us. With React, we do not interact with the DOM directly. We instead interact with a virtual DOM which React uses to construct the actual DOM.

The virtual DOM is made up of React elements (which we specify in JSX – more about that later) which

7

look similar to HTML elements but are actually Javascript objects. It is much faster to work with Javascript objects than with the DOM API directly. We make changes to the Javascript object (the virtual DOM) and React renders those changes for us as efficiently as possible.

### Asynchronous Operations

In times when we need to get or send data from/to the server, we send a request to the server. But these are mainly restricted to initial loading and necessary server-side operations like database operations. Besides these operations, we will not frequently need to request from the server. And if we do make server requests, we do it asynchronously, which means we still re-render the page instantly to the user and then wait for the new data to arrive and incorporate it and re-render only the required view when the data arrives; thus providing a fluid experience.

### Step by Step

In this book, I will teach you about React from scratch in step by step fashion. You will build an application where you can input search terms and receive the search results via GitHub RESTful api (fig. 1.1.1).

figure 1.1.1

In the end, you will also build a real-world application with full C.R.U.D. operations (fig. 1.1.2).

# Users

Add

| Username | Email | Edit | Delete |
|---|---|---|---|
| Ervin Howell | Shanna@melissa.tv | ☑ | ✖ |
| Clementine Bauch | Nathan@yesenia.net | ☑ | ✖ |
| Patricia Lebsack2 | Julianne.OConner@kory.org2 | ☑ | ✖ |
| Chelsey Dietrich | Lucio_Hettinger@annie.ca | ☑ | ✖ |
| Mrs. Dennis Schulist | Karley_Dach@jasper.info | ☑ | ✖ |
| Kurtis Weissnat | Telly.Hoeger@billy.biz | ☑ | ✖ |

figure 1.1.2

These are the patterns you see on a lot of real-world applications. In this book, you will learn how to implement these patterns with React.

Although this book covers techniques for developing single-page web applications with React, web browsers are not the only place React apps can run. React Native, released in 2015 allows us to develop iOS and Android native apps with React. And in the future, there is React VR, a framework for building interactive virtual reality apps that provides 360-degree experiences. We hope that this book will provide you with a strong base that you can build applications in React even beyond the web browser.

## Using ES6

In this book, we will be using ES6 syntax for our code. Both ES5 and ES6 are just Javascript, but ES6 provide more features for example:
- *const* (variable that cannot be changed),
- template strings. Instead of *console.log("Hello " + firstName)*, we can concatenate strings by surrounding them with ${}, i.e. *console.log(`Hello ${firstName}`)*
- arrow functions. In ES6, we can create functions without using the *function* keyword which simplifies the syntax.
- In declaring classes, ES6 can leverage on class features, object orientation as well as life cycle hook methods. Note that the ES5 way of declaring classes (*react.createClass*) is deprecated as of React 15.5.

This section is meant to address readers who have a bit of React development experience and are asking the question of whether to use ES6 or ES5. If you don't know what I am referring to, don't worry about it. We will go through the concepts in the course of this book. We will aim to use emerging Javascript whenever possible.

## 1.2 Thinking in Components

A React app is made up of components. For example, if we want to build a storefront module like what we see on Amazon, we can divide it into three components. The search bar component, sidebar component and products component.

A React component contains a JSX template that ultimately outputs HTML elements. It has its own data and logic to control the JSX template.

Components can also contain other components. For example, in *products* component where we display a list of products, we do so using multiple *product* components. Also, in each *product* component, we can have a *rating* component (fig. 1.2.1).

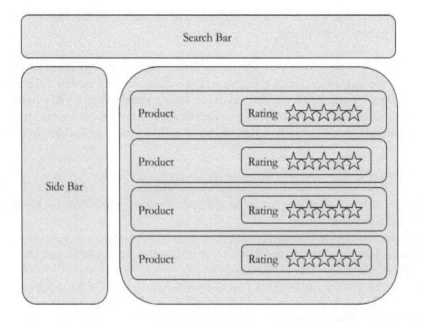

fig. 1.2.1

The benefit of such an architecture helps us to break up a large application into smaller manageable components. Plus, we can reuse components within the application or even in a different application. For example, we can re-use the rating component in a different application.

Below is an example of a component that displays a simple string 'Products'.

```
import React, { Component } from 'react';

class Products extends Component {
  render() {
    return (
      <div>
        <h2>
            Products
        </h2>
      </div>
    );
  }
}
```

As mentioned earlier, we define our React components using a HTML like syntax known as JSX. JSX is a syntax extension to Javascript. We use JSX to construct a virtual DOM with React elements. Facebook released JSX to provide a concise syntax for creating complex DOM trees with attributes. They hoped to make React more readable like HTML and XML.

This is the big picture of thinking in terms of components. As you progress through this book, you will see more of this in action.

## 1.3 Setting Up

*Installing Node*

First, we need to install NodeJS. NodeJS is a server-side language and we don't need it because we are not writing any server-side code. We mostly need it because of its *npm* or Node Package Manager. *npm* is very popular for managing dependencies of your applications. We will use *npm* to install other later tools that we need.

Get the latest version of NodeJS from *nodejs.org* and install it on your machine. Installing NodeJS should be pretty easy and straightforward.

To check if Node has been properly installed, type the below on your command line (Command Prompt on Windows or Terminal on Mac):

**node -v**

and you should see the node version displayed.

To see if npm is installed, type the below on your command line:

```
npm -v
```

and you should see the npm version displayed.

## Installing Create-React-App

'*create-react-app*' is the best way to start building a new React single page application. It sets up our development environment so that we can use the latest Javascript features and optimization for our app. It is a Command Line Interface tool that makes creating a new React project, adding files and other on-going development tasks like testing, bundling and deployment easier. It uses build tools like Babel and Webpack under the hood and provides a pleasant developer experience for us that we don't have to do any manual configurations for it.

To install '*create-react-app*' from the command line, run the following:

```
npm install -g create-react-app
```

## Code Editor

In this book, we will be using VScode (https://code.visualstudio.com/) which is a good, lightweight and cross-platform editor from Microsoft.

## Chrome Browser

We will be using Chrome as our browser. You can use other browsers but I highly recommend you use Chrome as we will be using Chrome developer tools in this book and I want to make sure you have the same experience as we go through the coding lessons.

## 1.4 Creating a New Project with *create-react-app*

First, in Terminal, navigate to the folder where you want to create your React project. Next, create a new React project and skeleton application with the following command,

```
create-react-app PROJECT_NAME
```

This will create your React project folder in that directory with three dependencies: React, ReactDOM and *react-scripts*. react-scripts is created by Facebook and it installs Babel, ESLint, Webpack and more so that we don't have to configure them manually.

When the folder is created, navigate to it by typing.

```
cd PROJECT_NAME
```

Next, type

```
npm start
```

The above command launches the server, watches your files and rebuilds the app as you make changes to those files. You can also run the *npm run build* command which creates a production-ready bundle that has been transpiled and minified.

Now, navigate to http://localhost:3000/ and your app greets you with the message displayed as in fig.1.4.1.

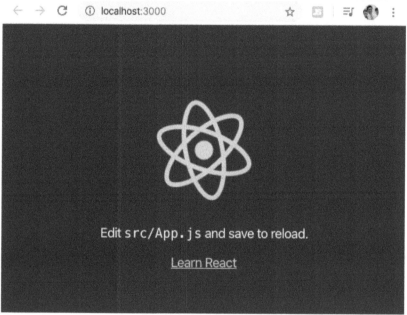

fig. 1.4.1

*Alternatively*

In the official documentation of *create-react-app* (https://reactjs.org/docs/create-a-new-react-app.html), it shows a different way of creating a project. I.e.:

```
npx create-react-app <project_name>
```

This is an alternate way of creating a React project without the need to run *npm install*. But why I didn't show this to you is because *npx* is a command line tool that only started to be installed in *npm* version 5.2 and higher. And it is likely that you have version 5.2 and earlier. If you want to use *npx*, you can upgrade your node version and then run *npx*. But in the end, there is no difference between both methods.

## Project File Review

Now let's look at the project files that have been created for us. When you open the project folder in VScode editor, you will find a couple of files (fig. 1.4.2).

fig. 1.4.2

We will not go through all the files as our focus is to get started with our first React app quickly, but we will briefly go through some of the more important files and folders.

Our app lives in the *src* folder. All React components, CSS styles, images (e.g. logo.svg) and anything else our app needs goes here. Any other files outside of this folder are meant to support building your app (the app folder is where we will work 99% of the time!). In the course of this book, you will come to appreciate the uses for the rest of the library files and folders.

In the *src* folder, we have *index.js* which is the main entry point for our app. In *index.js*, we render the *App* React element into the root DOM node. Applications built with just React usually have a single root DOM node.

*index.js*

```
import React from 'react';
import ReactDOM from 'react-dom';
import './index.css';
```

```
import App from './App';
import * as serviceWorker from './serviceWorker';

ReactDOM.render(
  <React.StrictMode>
    <App />
  </React.StrictMode>,
  document.getElementById('root')
);


serviceWorker.unregister();
```

In *index.js*, we import both React and ReactDOM which we need to work with React in the browser. React is the library for creating views. ReactDOM is the library used to render the UI in the browser. The two libraries were split into two packages for version 0.14 and the purpose for splitting is to allow for components to be shared between the web version of React and React Native, thus supporting rendering for a variety of platforms.

*index.js* imports *index.css*, App component and *serviceWorker* with the following lines.

```
import './index.css';
import App from './App';
import * as serviceWorker from './serviceWorker';
```

It then renders App with:

```
ReactDOM.render(
  <React.StrictMode>
    <App />
  </React.StrictMode>,
  document.getElementById('root')
);
```

The last line `serviceWorker.unregister()` has comments:

```
// If you want your app to work offline and load faster, you can change
// unregister() to register() below. Note this comes with some pitfalls.
// Learn more about service workers: https://bit.ly/CRA-PWA
```

*serviceWorker.register()* is meant to create progressive web apps (PWA) catered more for mobile React Native apps to work offline. This however is out of the scope of this book and we can safely leave the code as `serviceWorker.unregister()` for now.

*App.js*

```
import React from 'react';
import logo from './logo.svg';
import './App.css';

function App() {
  return (
    <div className="App">
      <header className="App-header">
        <img src={logo} className="App-logo" alt="logo" />
        <p>
          Edit <code>src/App.js</code> and save to reload.
        </p>
        <a
          className="App-link"
          href="https://reactjs.org"
          target="_blank"
          rel="noopener noreferrer"
        >
          Learn React
        </a>
      </header>
    </div>
  );
}

export default App;
```

Note: any element that has an HTML class attribute is using *className* for that property instead of *class*. Since *class* is a reserved word in Javascript, we have to use *className* to define the class attribute of an HTML element.

In the above, we have a functional-based component called *App*. Every React application has at least one component: the root component, named *App* in *App.js*. The App component controls the view through the JSX template it returns:

```
  return (
      <div className="App">
          ...
      </div>
  );
```

16

A component has to return a **single** React element. In our case, *App* returns a single <*div* />. The element can be a representation of a native DOM component, such as <*div* />, or another composite component that you've defined yourself. We will dwell more on this in the next chapter.

The funny tag syntax returned by the component is not HTML but JSX. JSX is a syntax extension to Javascript. We use it to describe what the UI should be like. Like HTML, in JSX, an element's type is specified with a tag. The tag's attributes represent the properties. Also, the element's children can be added between the opening and closing tags.

Components can either be *functional* based or *class* based. We will talk more on this later, but as a starter, what we have in *App* is a functional-based component as seen from its header *function App()*.

We also have the *package.json* file and *node_modules* folder:

*package.json* is the node package configuration which lists the third-party packages our project uses.

*node_modules* folder is created by Node.js and puts all third-party modules listed in *package.json* in it.

## 1.5 Editing our first React Component

'create-react-app' created the first React functional-based component for us in *App.js*. Now, we will convert our functional-based component to a class-based component.

Open App.js and change it to the following:

```
import React, { Component } from 'react';

class App extends Component {
  render() {
    return (
      <div>
        <h1>
        My First React App!
        </h1>
      </div>
    );
  }
}

export default App;
```

What we have above is a class-based component, as evident from the *class* declaration. Similar to the functional-based component we saw earlier, the class-based component also returns a JSX template but this time through its *render()* method. In a React class-based component, implementing the *render()* method is required. Like the *return* of a functional-based component, *render()* should return a single React element.

Additionally, in a class-based component, we can define application logic to interact with the view through properties and methods. For now, our root app component class has no properties or methods.

When you run your app, you should see something like:

# My First React App!

Now in App.js, try changing "My First React App!" to "My Second React App". Notice that the browser reloads automatically with the revised title. Because React compiler is running in the 'watch' mode, it detects that there is a file change and re-compiles the file. In the Chrome browser, the app gets refreshed automatically so you don't have to refresh the page every time your code changes.

By now, you would probably have a question. So, should I use a functional-based component or class-based one? I come to that in chapter twelve as explaining them to you now would not be meaningful. What I aim to do first is get you familiar first with class-based components. And later on, when you understand class-based components better, we can then make a more meaningful contrast with functional-based components and how React Hooks fit into the whole picture.

As a precursor, this book largely focuses on React development through class components except in the last chapter. I have written a separate book ("Beginning React with Hooks", *https://www.amazon.com/dp/B088ZT9P36/*) which brings you through React development using function components.

If you have bought this book but prefer to journey in React development with function components, don't worry. Just drop me a mail at support@i-ducate.com and I will give you a complimentary copy of "Beginning React with Hooks" as a way of expressing thanks to you for supporting me.

## Summary

In this chapter, we have been introduced to the core building blocks of React apps which are components. We have also been introduced to the React development experience which is creating a new React project with *create-react-app*. *create-react-app* provides internal compilation which automatically generates our app for us that we can view on the browser. It is a great tool for developers, whether beginner or advanced. Keep an eye on its changes in GitHub as more functionality is added to it. In the next chapter, we will begin implementing a React app.

# CHAPTER 2: CREATING AND USING COMPONENTS

In the previous chapter, you learned about the core building blocks of React apps, components. In this chapter, we will implement a custom class-based component from scratch to have an idea of what it is like to build a React app.

## 2.1 Creating our First Component

In VScode, open the project folder that you have created in chapter 1. We first add a new file in the *src* folder and call it *Products.js* (fig. 2.1.1).

figure 2.1.1

Note the naming convention of the file; we capitalize the first letter of the component *Products* followed by *.js*.

Type out the below code into *Products.js*:

```
import React, { Component } from 'react';

class Products extends Component {
  render() {
    return (
      <div>
        <h2>
            Products
```

```
        </h2>
      </div>
    );
  }
}
```

```
export default Products;
```

*Code Explanation*

*import React, { Component } from 'react'* imports the Component class from 'react' library which we use to extend.

In the *render* method, we specify the JSX that will be inserted into the DOM as HTML when the component's view is rendered. Our current html markup is:

```
<div>
  <h2>
        Products
  </h2>
</div>
```

Note that components must return a single root element. If we have:

```
render() {
  return (
    <h2>
          Products
    </h2>
    <h2>
          Courses
    </h2>
  );
}
```

The above will throw an error. So, we typically add a *<div>* to contain all internal elements like:

```
render() {
  return (
    <div>
      <h2>
            Products
      </h2>
      <h2>
            Courses
```

```
      </h2>
    </div>
  );
}
```

Lastly, *export default Products* makes this component available for other files in our application to import it.

With these simple lines of code, we have just built our first React component!

## 2.2 Using our Created Component

Now, go back to *App.js*. Notice that the contents of *App.js* is very similar to *Products.js*.

Remember that App component is the root of our application. It is the view component that controls our entire app or page.

Now, import and add *<Products />* to the template as shown below.

```
import React, { Component } from 'react';
import Products from './Products';

class App extends Component {
  render() {
    return (
      <div>
        <h1>My First React App!</h1>
        <Products />
      </div>
    );
  }
}

export default App;
```

*Code Explanation*

We have just referred to another component from a component. We can also render *Products* many times:

```
  render() {
    return (
      <div>
        <h1>My First React App!</h1>
        <Products />
        <Products />
        <Products />
```

```
      </div>
    );
  }
```

Now save the file and go to your browser. You should see the Products component markup displayed with the message:

# My First React App!

## Products

Notice that we also have to first import our *Products* Component using

```
import Products from './Products';
```

For custom components that we have defined, we need to specify their path in the file system. Since App component and Products Component are in the same folder app, we use './' which means start searching from the current folder followed by the name of the component, *Products* (without *.js* extension).

*<Products />* here acts as a custom tag which allows us to extend or control our virtual DOM. In this way, we can design custom components that are not part of standard JSX.

## 2.3 Embedding Expressions in JSX

You can embed Javascript expressions in JSX by wrapping it in curly braces. For example, we can define functions, properties and render them in the output. The below App component has a function *formatName* which takes in a *user* object which holds *firstName* and *lastName* properties. We then call *formatName* in *render* within the curly braces.

```
class App extends Component {

  formatName(user){
    return user.firstName + ' ' + user.lastName;
  }

  render() {
    const user ={
      firstName:'Greg',
      lastName:'Lim'
    };

    return (
      <div>
```

```
        <h1>Hello, {this.formatName(user)}</h1>
      </div>
    );
  }
}
```

If the value of the property in the *user* object changes, the view will be automatically refreshed.

You can also use curly braces to embed a Javascript expression in an attribute for example:

```
<img src={user.imageUrl}></img>
```

## Displaying a List

We will illustrate using properties further by displaying a list of products in *Products*. In Products.js, add the codes shown in bold below:

```
import React, { Component } from 'react';

class Products extends Component {

  render() {
    const products = ["Learning React","Pro React","Beginning React"];
    const listProducts = products.map((product) =>
        <li key={product.toString()}>{product}</li>
    );

    return (
      <div>
        <ul>{listProducts}</ul>
      </div>
    );
  }
}

export default Products;
```

Navigate to your browser and you should see the result in fig. 2.3.1

- Learning React
- Pro React
- Beginning React

fig. 2.3.1

25

*Code Explanation*

```
const products = ["Learning React","Pro React","Beginning React"];
```

First, in *render*, we declare an array *products* in Products Component which contains the names of the products that we are listing.

```
const listProducts = products.map((product) =>
    <li key={product.toString()}>{product}</li>
);
```

We next define an ES6 arrow function

```
(product) => <li key={product.toString()}>{product}</li>
```

that returns an *<li>* element for each product. We then pass in this function into *map* which loops through each element, calls the function that returns an *<li></li>* element for each product, and we are returned a new array of elements which we assign to *listProducts*.

```
return (
  <div>
     <ul>{listProducts}</ul>
  </div>
);
```

We include the entire *listProducts* array inside a <ul> element, and render it to the DOM:

Note that we have provided a *key* attribute for our list items. A "key" is a special string attribute you need to include when creating lists of elements. If you don't provide this attribute, you will still have your items listed but a warning message will be displayed. Keys help React identify which items have changed, are added, or are removed. Keys should ideally be strings that uniquely identify a list item among its siblings. Most often, you would use IDs from your data as keys. But in our case, we do not yet have an id. Thus we use the *product.toString()*. You should always use keys as much as possible because bugs creep into your code (especially when you do operations like deleting, editing individual list items – you delete/edit the wrong item!) when you do not use it.

## Summary

You have learned a lot in this chapter. If you get stuck while following the code or if you would like to get the sample code we have used in this chapter, visit my GitHub repository at
https://github.com/greglim81/react-chapter2 or contact me at support@i-ducate.com.
In this chapter, we created our first component. We created a ProductsComponent that retrieves product data from an array and later renders that data on the page.

# CHAPTER 3: BINDINGS, PROPS, STATE AND EVENTS

In this chapter, we will explore displaying data by binding controls in a JSX template to properties of a React component, how to apply css classes on styles dynamically, how to use the component state and how to handle events raised from DOM elements.

## 3.1 CSS Class Binding

In the following code, we show a button in our view using *react-bootstrap* to make our button look more professional. React-Bootstrap (https://react-bootstrap.github.io) is a library of reusable front-end components that contain JSX based templates to help build user interface components (like forms, buttons, icons) for web applications.

*Installing React-Bootstrap*

In the Terminal, run:

```
npm install react-bootstrap bootstrap
```

Next, in the existing project from chapter two, we need to reference *bootstrap.css* in *index.html*. Go to 'react-bootstrap.github.io', under 'Getting Started', 'CSS', copy the stylesheet link:

```
<!-- it should look something like the below, but please copy the latest link from
the react bootstrap documentation -->

<link rel="stylesheet"
href="https://maxcdn.bootstrapcdn.com/bootstrap/latest/css/bootstrap.min.css">
```

and add it to index.html in your project's *public* folder to get the latest styles.

To check if we have installed react-bootstrap correctly, we add a button into our App component by adding the lines in bold:

```
import React, { Component } from 'react';
import Products from './Products';
import { Button } from 'react-bootstrap';

class App extends Component {
```

```
    render() {
      return (
        <div>
          <Products />
          <Button>Default</Button>
        </div>
      );
    }
}

export default App;
```

If you have successfully linked your react-bootstrap class, you should get your button displayed like in fig. 3.1.1.

# My First React App!

- Learning React
- Pro React
- Beginning React

fig. 3.1.1

There are times when we want to use different css classes on an element. For example, if we add the 'danger' button style as shown below:

```
<Button variant="danger">Default</Button>
```

we get the below button style.

# My First React App!

- Learning React
- Pro React
- Beginning React

And if I want to disable the button by applying the *disabled* class, I can do the following

```
<Button variant="primary" disabled>Default</Button>
```

More information of styles of *button* and other components are available at the React Bootstrap site under 'Components'.

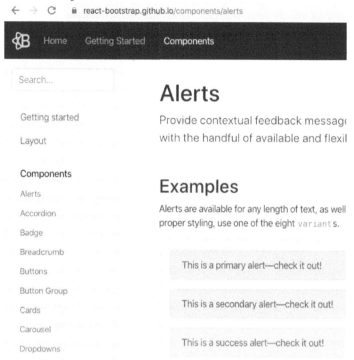

## Disabling Button on Condition

Now, suppose I want to disable the button based on some condition, we can do the below:

```
render() {
  const isValid = true;

  return (
    <div>
      <Products />
      <Button variant="primary" disabled={!isValid}>Default</Button>
    </div>
  );
}
```

That is, when *isValid = false* the *disabled* css class will be applied, making the button unclickable. If *isValid = true* the *disabled* css class will not be applied, making the button clickable.

## 3.2 Props

We can pass data into a component by passing in a single object called 'props'. The 'props' object contains JSX attributes. For example, suppose we want to display a list of products with its rating. We will need to assign the rating value to our rating component beforehand. We can do something like: *<Rating rating="4"/>* to display a rating of 4 stars.

'props' will contain the value of 4 assigned to the *rating* attribute. To access 'props' in our Rating component, we use *props.rating*.

For example, in Rating.js (our Rating component), the below code renders the rating value on the page.

```
import React, { Component } from 'react';

class Rating extends Component {

  render() {
    return (
      <div>
        <h1>Rating: {this.props.rating}</h1>
      </div>
    );
  }
}

export default Rating;
```

In App.js, add in the codes below into *render()*:

```
  render() {
    return (
      <div>
        <Rating rating="1"/>
        <Rating rating="2"/>
        <Rating rating="3"/>
        <Rating rating="4"/>
        <Rating rating="5"/>
      </div>
    );
  }
```

Remember to import Rating by adding the following in App.js:

```
import Rating from './Rating';
```

If you run your app now, it should display something like:

# Rating: 1
# Rating: 2
# Rating: 3
# Rating: 4
# Rating: 5

To recap, we call *render()* in App.js with `<Rating rating="1"/>`. React calls the Rating component with { *rating: '1'* } as the props. Our Rating component returns a `<h1>Rating: 1</h1>` element as the result and React DOM updates the DOM.

In this example, our props object contains only one attribute. But it can contain multiple and even complex objects as attribute(s). We will illustrate this later in the book.

## Props are Read-Only

Note that when we access props in our components, we must never modify them. Our functions must always be 'pure' – which means that we do not attempt to change our inputs and must always return the same result for the same inputs. In other words, props are read-only. For example, the below function is impure and not allowed:

```
render() {
  return (
    <div>
      <h1>Rating: {this.props.rating++}</h1>
    </div>
  );
}
```

We can use React flexibly but it has a single strict rule: that all React components must act like pure functions concerning their props. So how do we make our application UI dynamic and change over time? Later on, we will introduce the concept of 'state', where we use it to change our output over time in response to user actions or network responses without violating this rule.

But first, we will improve the look of our rating component by showing rating stars like what we see in Amazon.com instead of showing the rating value numerically. A user can click select from a rating of one star to five stars. We will implement this as a component and reuse it in many places. For now, don't worry about calling a server or any other logic. We just want to implement the UI first.

## 3.3 Improving the Look

To show rating stars instead of just number values, we will use the React Icons library from https://react-icons.github.io/react-icons/ which provides popular icons in our React project. Install react icons by running:

```
npm install react-icons --save
```

We will be using the IoIosStarOutline and IoIosStar ionicons:
(https://react-icons.github.io/react-icons/icons?name=io).

IoIosStarOutline          IoIosStar

To include them in our React project, add the below codes in **bold** into Rating component:

```
import React, { Component } from 'react';
import { IoIosStar, IoIosStarOutline } from 'react-icons/io'

class Rating extends Component {

  render() {
    return (
      <div>
        <h1>Rating: {this.props.rating}</h1>
        {this.props.rating >= 1 ? (
            <IoIosStar />
        ) : (
            <IoIosStarOutline />
        )}
        {this.props.rating >= 2 ? (
            <IoIosStar />
        ) : (
            <IoIosStarOutline />
        )}
        {this.props.rating >= 3 ? (
```

```
        <IoIosStar />
    ) : (
        <IoIosStarOutline />
    )}
    {this.props.rating >= 4 ? (
        <IoIosStar />
    ) : (
        <IoIosStarOutline />
    )}
    {this.props.rating >= 5 ? (
        <IoIosStar />
    ) : (
        <IoIosStarOutline />
    )}
    </div>
    );
  }
}

export default Rating;
```

*Code Explanation*

We first import the *IosIosStar* and *IoIosStarOutline* icons from 'react-icons/io' with

```
import { IoIosStar, IoIosStarOutline } from 'react-icons/io'
```

In the *render* method, we add the *IosIosStar* and *IoIosStarOutline* icons with:

```
{this.props.rating >= 1 ? (
    <IoIosStar />
) : (
    <IoIosStarOutline />
)}
```

*Conditional Rendering*

We conditionally render an IosIosStar (filled star) if the this.props.rating is >= 1. Else, render IosIosStarOutline (empty star). We will dwell more on the If-Else conditional code in chapter 5.

The above code is for the first star. The remaining similar repetitions are for the four remaining stars. However, note the change in value of each condition depending on which star it is. For example, the second star's condition should be

```
{this.props.rating >= 2 ? (
    <IoIosStar />
) : (
    <IoIosStarOutline />
)}
```

The second star should be empty if the rating is less than two. It should be filled if the rating is more than or equal to two. The same goes for the third, fourth and fifth star.

*Running your App*

When we run our app, we get the icons displayed:

# Rating: 1

★☆☆☆☆

# Rating: 2

★★☆☆☆

# Rating: 3

★★★☆☆

# Rating: 4

★★★★☆

# Rating: 5

★★★★★

## 3.4 Adding Local State to a Component

Now, suppose we want our user to be able to change the rating by clicking on the specified star. How do we make our rating component render in response to a user click? And considering that we cannot modify this.props.rating?

This is where we have to add 'state' to our Rating component. State is similar to props, but it is private and fully controlled by the component. State manages data that will change within a component.

Whenever state changes, the UI is re-rendered to reflect those changes. We often refer to this as the component or local state. To add local state to our component, we first add a class constructor that assigns the initial state:

```
class Rating extends Component {

  constructor(props) {
    super(props);
    this.state = {rating: this.props.rating};
  }

    ...
```

Note how *props* is passed to the base constructor with *super(props)*. We should always call the base constructor with *props. props* in turn are sent to the superclass by invoking *super()*. The superclass is *React.Component*. Invoking *super* initializes the component instance and *React.Component* decorates that instance with functionality that includes state management. After invoking super, we can initialize our component's state variables.

Just like *props*, realize that *this.state* is a single object that can contain one or more attributes. We initialize our initial state in the constructor. Our current state is an object containing a single attribute *rating* which is assigned the value from this.*props.rating*. You can also initialize rating in state to 0 by default with  *this.state = {rating: 0};*

Next, replace *this.props.rating* with *this.state.rating* in the *render()* method:

```
render() {
    return (
      <div>
        <h1>Rating: {this.state.rating}</h1>
        {this.state.rating >= 1 ? (
            <IoIosStar />
        ) : (
            <IoIosStarOutline />
        )}
        {this.state.rating >= 2 ? (
            <IoIosStar />
        ) : (
            <IoIosStarOutline />
        )}
        {this.state.rating >= 3 ? (
            <IoIosStar />
        ) : (
```

```
            <IoIosStarOutline />
        )}
        {this.state.rating >= 4 ? (
            <IoIosStar />
        ) : (
            <IoIosStarOutline />
        )}
        {this.state.rating >= 5 ? (
            <IoIosStar />
        ) : (
            <IoIosStarOutline />
        )}
      </div>
    );
  }
```

If you run your app now, it should display the Rating component just as the same as before. The purpose of why we use *state.rating* instead of *props.rating* will become more apparent in the following sections.

## 3.5 Handling Events with States

Next, we want to assign a rating depending on which star the user has clicked. To do so, our component needs to handle the click event. Handling events with React components is very similar to handling events on DOM elements. However, with JSX we pass a function as the event handler, rather than a string. For example, to make our rating component handle user clicks, we add the following in the *render* method:

```
render() {
  return (
    <div>
      <h1>Rating: {this.state.rating}</h1>
      {this.state.rating >= 1 ? (
          <IoIosStar onClick={this.handleClick.bind(this,1)}/>
      ) : (
          <IoIosStarOutline onClick={this.handleClick.bind(this,1)}/>
      )}
      {this.state.rating >= 2 ? (
          <IoIosStar onClick={this.handleClick.bind(this,2)}/>
      ) : (
          <IoIosStarOutline onClick={this.handleClick.bind(this,2)}/>
      )}
      {this.state.rating >= 3 ? (
```

```
        <IoIosStar onClick={this.handleClick.bind(this,3)}/>
    ) : (
        <IoIosStarOutline onClick={this.handleClick.bind(this,3)}/>
    )}
    {this.state.rating >= 4 ? (
        <IoIosStar onClick={this.handleClick.bind(this,4)}/>
    ) : (
        <IoIosStarOutline onClick={this.handleClick.bind(this,4)}/>
    )}
    {this.state.rating >= 5 ? (
        <IoIosStar onClick={this.handleClick.bind(this,5)}/>
    ) : (
        <IoIosStarOutline onClick={this.handleClick.bind(this,5)}/>
    )}
    </div>
  );
}
```

In each star, we pass in the *handleClick* function as the event handler with *ratingValue* attribute to the *onClick* event. For example, we have `onClick={this.handleClick.bind(this,1)}` to assign a rating of one if a user clicks on this star. We then change the value of the argument to *handleClick* function depending on which star it is. The second star's *handleClick* should be `onClick={this.handleClick.bind(this,2)}`. So, when a user clicks on the second star, the *handleClick* method is called with property *rating* of value two. When a user clicks on the third star, the *handleClick* method is called with property *rating* of value three and so on.

Next, we also need to bind the *handleClick* function to our component with `this.handleClick.bind(this,<value>)` as class methods in Javascript are not bound by default.

We then define the *handleClick* function:

```
handleClick(ratingValue){
   this.setState({rating:ratingValue});
}
```

Note that in *handleClick*, we CANNOT modify our state directly like *this.state.rating = ratingValue*. Whenever we want to modify our state, we must use the *setState* method which we automatically calls the *render()* method which re-renders our component thus showing the updated value on to the view.

*Running your App*

When you run your app now, you should be able to see your ratings and also adjust their values by clicking on the specified star (figure 3.5.1).

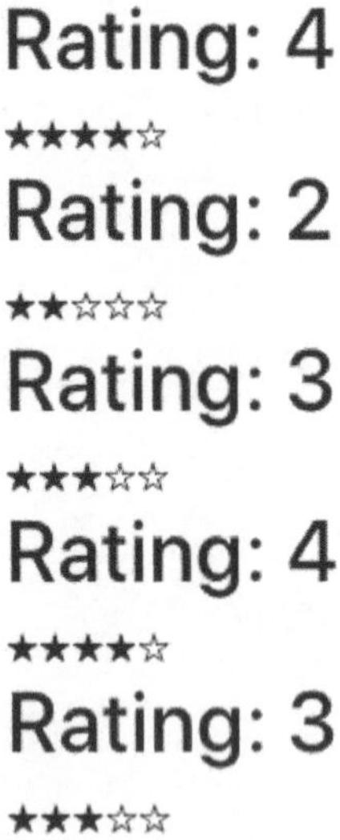

# Rating: 4

★★★★☆

# Rating: 2

★★☆☆☆

# Rating: 3

★★★☆☆

# Rating: 4

★★★★☆

# Rating: 3

★★★☆☆

fig. 3.5.1

Note that we have five different rating components each having their own local state. Each updates independently. Each rating component does not have access to another rating component's state. But each rating component may choose to pass its state down as props to its own child components in a top-down fashion.

*Summary*

In this chapter, we learned about CSS class binding, props, adding local state and handling events. In the next chapter, we will see how to put multiple components together in an application.

Visit my GitHub repository at https://github.com/greglim81/react-chapter3 if you have not already have the full source code for this chapter or contact me at support@i-ducate.com if you encounter any errors with your code.

# Chapter 4: Working with Components

In this chapter, we will learn more about using components, how to reuse them and put them together in an application. Execute the codes in the following sections in your existing project from chapter three.

## 4.1 Styles

On top of the components provided by React-bootstrap, we can further modify them with our own css styles required by our component. These *styles* are scoped only to your component. They won't effect to the outer DOM or other components.

To illustrate, suppose we want our filled stars to be orange, in Rating.js we add the following in **bold** after *export default Rating.*

```
...
export default Rating;

const styles={
  starStyle:{
    color: 'orange'
  }
}
```

We have created a new object under the Rating component called *styles* and in it, we provide the styling specifications. If required, you can further specify other styling properties like *height*, *backgroundColor*, *fontSize* etc.

To apply this style, add the below *style* attribute in the *<div>* containing the rating component.

```
render() {
  return (
    <div style={styles.starStyle}>
      <h1>Rating: {this.state.rating}</h1>
        ...
```

When we run our application, we will see our filled stars with the orange css applied to it (fig. 4.1.1).

★☆☆☆☆
★★☆☆☆
★★★☆☆
★★★★☆
★★★★★

figure. 4.1.1

## 4.2 Example Application

We will reuse the rating component that we have made and implement a product listing like in figure 4.2.1.

### Product 1

May 31, 2016

★★★★☆2

Lorem ipsum dolor sit amet, consectetur adipiscing elit. Aenean porttitor, tel enim ex faucibus nulla, id rutrum ligula purus sit amet mauris.

### Product 2

October 31, 2016

★★☆☆☆12

Lorem ipsum dolor sit amet, consectetur adipiscing elit. Aenean porttitor, tel enim ex faucibus nulla, id rutrum ligula purus sit amet mauris.

### Product 3

July 30, 2016

★★★★★2

Lorem ipsum dolor sit amet, consectetur adipiscing elit. Aenean porttitor, tel enim ex faucibus nulla, id rutrum ligula purus sit amet mauris.

fig. 4.2.1

This is like the list of products on Amazon. For each product, we have an image, the product name, the product release date, the rating component and the number of ratings it has.

In *src*, create a new component file *Product.js* that contains the Product Component. This component will be used to render one product. Fill in the file with the below code.

```
import React, { Component } from 'react';

class Product extends Component {

  constructor(props){
    super(props);
```

```
  }

  render() {
    return (
    );
  }
}

export default Product;
```

Now, how do we get our template to render each product listing like in figure 4.2.1? We use the *media object* in react-bootstrap. Go to react-bootstrap.github.io, in 'Layout', click on 'Media' (fig. 4.2.2) and copy the JSX markup there into the *render* method of Product Component.

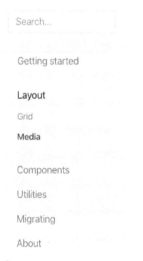

# Media objects

The media object helps build complex and repetitive components (e.g. blog comments, tweets, the like and more) where some media is positioned alongside content that doesn't wrap around said media. Plus, it does this with only two required classes thanks to flexbox. Below is an example of a single media object. Only two classes are required—the wrapping Media and the Media.Body around your content. Optional padding and margin can be controlled through spacing utilities.

Search...

Getting started

**Layout**

Grid

**Media**

Components

Utilities

Migrating

About

### Media Heading

Cras sit amet nibh libero, in gravida nulla. Nulla vel metus scelerisque ante sollicitudin commodo. Cras purus odio, vestibulum in vulputate at, tempus viverra turpis. Fusce condimentum nunc ac nisi vulputate fringilla. Donec lacinia congue felis in faucibus.

fig. 4.2.2

Next in *render*, we use *props* to assign values of our product into our JSX. Type in the below codes in bold into the template.

```
  render() {
    return (
      <div>
        <Media>
          <img
              width={64}
              height={64}
              className="mr-3"
              src={this.props.data.imageUrl}
```

41

```
            alt="Image"
        />
      <Media.Body>
        <h5>{this.props.data.productName}</h5>
        { this.props.data.releasedDate }
        <Rating
              rating={this.props.data.rating}
              numOfReviews={this.props.data.numOfReviews}
        />
        <p>{this.props.data.description}</p>
      </Media.Body>
    </Media>
  </div>
);
}
```

With the above code, our product component is expecting a *props data* object with the fields: *imageUrl*, *productName*, *releasedDate* and *description*.

We have also added our rating component that expects input rating and number of reviews.

```
<Rating
      rating={this.props.data.rating}
      numOfReviews={this.props.data.numOfReviews}
/>
```

Our rating component currently only has *rating-value* as input. Add {*this.props.numOfReviews*} at the end of Rating.js to display the number of reviews beside the rating stars.

Lastly in Product.js, make sure that you have imported *Rating* and *Media*:

```
import Rating from './Rating';
import { Media } from 'react-bootstrap';
```

*Products.js*

Next in Products.js, add a method *getProducts* that is responsible for returning a list of products. Type in the below code (or copy it from my GitHub repository https://github.com/greglim81/react-chapter4) into Products.js.

```
getProducts() {
  return [
  {
      imageUrl: "http://loremflickr.com/150/150?random=1",
      productName: "Product 1",
      releasedDate: "May 31, 2016",
```

```
            description: "Lorem ipsum dolor sit amet, consectetur adipiscing elit.
Aenean porttitor, tellus laoreet venenatis facilisis, enim ex faucibus nulla, id
rutrum ligula purus sit amet mauris. ",
            rating: 4,
            numOfReviews: 2
        },
        {

            imageUrl: "http://loremflickr.com/150/150?random=2",
            productName: "Product 2",
            releasedDate: "October 31, 2016",
            description: "Lorem ipsum dolor sit amet, consectetur adipiscing elit.
Aenean porttitor, tellus laoreet venenatis facilisis, enim ex faucibus nulla, id
rutrum ligula purus sit amet mauris. ",
            rating: 2,
            numOfReviews: 12
        },
        {

            imageUrl: "http://loremflickr.com/150/150?random=3",
            productName: "Product 3",
            releasedDate: "July 30, 2016",
            description: "Lorem ipsum dolor sit amet, consectetur adipiscing elit.
Aenean porttitor, tellus laoreet venenatis facilisis, enim ex faucibus nulla, id
rutrum ligula purus sit amet mauris. ",
            rating: 5,
            numOfReviews: 2
        }];
    }
```

Notice that in our class, we currently hardcode an array of product objects. Later on, we will explore how to receive data from a server.

For *imageUrl*, we use http://loremflickr.com/150/150?random=1 to render a random image 150 pixels by 150 pixels. For multiple product images, we change the query string parameter *random=2, 3,4* and so on to get a different random image.

The *getProducts* method will be called in our Products Component constructor. We return the results from *getProducts* to a *products* variable. Add the codes below in **bold** into Products.js.

*Products.js*

```
import React, { Component } from 'react';
import Product from './Product';

class Products extends Component {

  products;

  constructor(props) {
```

```
    super(props);
    this.products = this.getProducts();
  }

getProducts() {
  return [...]

render() {
  const listProducts = this.products.map((product) =>
      <Product key={product.productName} data={product} />
  );

  return (
    <div>
      <ul>{listProducts}</ul>
    </div>
  );
  }
}
}

export default Products;
```

The code on *render()* is similar to the one in chapter three where we loop through the names in *products* array to list them. This time however, our element is not just simple strings but an object which itself contains several Product attributes.

The function we define now returns a <Product> component with the product *data* object as input for each product. Each *data* object input provides Product component with values from properties *imageUrl*, *productName*, *releasedDate*, *description*, *rating* and *numOfReviews*.

We pass in this function into *map* which loops through each element, calls the function that returns a <Product /> component for each product, and we are returned a new array of Product components which we assign to *listProducts*.

Note that we have provided *productName* as *key* attribute for our list items. Remember that "key" is a special string attribute which help React identify which items have changed, are added, or are removed. Because *productName* might not be unique, I will leave it to you as an exercise on how you can use *Product id* which uniquely identifies a product to be the key instead.

Lastly in *App.js*, make sure you render your *Products* component:

```
import React from 'react';
import Products from './Products';

function App() {
```

```
  return (
    <div className="App">
        <Products />
    </div>
  );
}


export default App;
```

Save all your files and you should have your application running fine like in figure 4.2.3.

### Product 1
May 31, 2016
★★★★☆ 2

Lorem ipsum dolor sit amet, consectetur adipiscing elit. Aenean porttitor, tel enim ex faucibus nulla, id rutrum ligula purus sit amet mauris.

### Product 2
October 31, 2016
★★☆☆☆ 12

Lorem ipsum dolor sit amet, consectetur adipiscing elit. Aenean porttitor, tel enim ex faucibus nulla, id rutrum ligula purus sit amet mauris.

### Product 3
July 30, 2016
★★★★★ 2

Lorem ipsum dolor sit amet, consectetur adipiscing elit. Aenean porttitor, tel enim ex faucibus nulla, id rutrum ligula purus sit amet mauris.

figure 4.2.3

## Summary

In this chapter, we illustrate how to modify css styles taken from *react-bootstrap* and reusing components to put them together in our example Product Listing application.

Contact me at support@i-ducate.com if you encounter any issues or visit my GitHub repository at https://github.com/greglim81/react-chapter4 for the full source code of this chapter.

# CHAPTER 5: CONDITIONAL RENDERING

In this chapter, we will explore functionality to give us more control in rendering HTML via JSX.

## 5.1 Inline If with && Operator

Suppose you want to show or hide part of a view depending on some condition. For example, we have earlier displayed our list of products. But if there are no products to display, we want to display a message like "No products to display" on the page. To do so, in Product.js of the existing project from chapter four, add the codes in **bold**:

```
render() {
  const listProducts = this.products.map((product) =>
      <Product key={product.productName} data={product} />
  );

  return (
    <div>
      {listProducts.length > 0 &&
        <ul>{listProducts}</ul>
      }
      {listProducts.length == 0 &&
        <ul>No Products to display</ul>
      }
    </div>
  );
}
```

Now when we rerun our app, we should see the products displayed as same as before. But if we comment out our hard-coded data in Product.js and return an empty array instead, we should get the following message.

No Products to display

*Code Explanation*

```
return (

    {listProducts.length > 0 &&
      <ul>{listProducts}</ul>
    }
```

Remember that we can embed any expression in JSX by wrapping them in curly braces. Thus, we can use the Javascript logical && operator to conditionally show *listProducts* if *listProducts.length > 0*. If the condition is true, i.e. *listProducts.length > 0* is true, the element right after && which is *<ul>{listProducts}</ul>* will appear in the output. If it is false, React will ignore and skip it.

The following expression however evaluates to false and therefore, we don't display the message.

```
{listProducts.length == 0 &&
   <ul>No Products to display</ul>
}
```

When we return an empty array however, *"products.length > 0"* evaluates to false and we do not render the list of products. Instead we display the "No products to display message".

## Inline If-Else with Conditional Operator

The above code can also be implemented with if/else by using the Javascript conditional operator *condition ? true : false*. We have actually previously used this to conditionally render either a filled star or empty one.

```
render() {
  const listProducts = this.products.map((product) =>
      <Product key={product.productName} data={product} />
  );

  return (
    <div>
      {listProducts.length > 0 ? (
          <ul>{listProducts}</ul>
      ) : (
        <ul>No Products to display</ul>
      )}
    </div>
  );
}
```

*Code Explanation*

```
{listProducts.length > 0 ? (
    <ul>{listProducts}</ul>
) : (
  <ul>No Products to display</ul>
)}
```

48

The above code is saying, "If *listProducts* length is > 0, then show `<ul>{listProducts}</ul>`. Otherwise (else) show what follows ':' which is `<ul>No Products to display</ul>`.

## 5.2 *props.children*

Sometimes, we need to insert content into our component from the outside. For example, we want to implement a component that wraps a bootstrap jumbotron. A bootstrap jumbotron (fig. 5.2.1) as defined on getbootstrap.com is "A lightweight, flexible component that can optionally extend the entire viewport to showcase key content on your site."

# Hello, world!

This is a simple hero unit, a simple jumbotron-style component for calling extra attention to featured content or information.

fig. 5.2.1

Here is an implementation of the bootstrap jumbotron component.

```
import React, { Component } from 'react';

import { Jumbotron, Button } from 'react-bootstrap';

class JumboTronComponent extends Component {

  render() {
    return (
      <div>
        <Jumbotron>
            <h1>Hello, world!</h1>
            <p>This is a simple hero unit, a simple jumbotron-style component for
calling extra attention to featured content or information.</p>
            <p><Button variant="primary">Learn more</Button></p>
        </Jumbotron>
      </div>
    );
  }
}

export default JumboTronComponent;
```

The markup above can be obtained from:
https://react-bootstrap.github.io/components.html#jumbotron.

The jumbotron component is called in App.js using,

```
import React, { Component } from 'react';
import JumboTronComponent from './JumboTronComponent';

class App extends Component {
  render() {
    return (
      <div>
        <JumboTronComponent />
      </div>
    );
  }
}
```

```
export default App;
```

To supply content to the jumbotron component, we can use *attributes* like:

```
<JumboTronComponent body='...' />
```

This is not ideal however. For we probably want to write a lengthier html markup here like,

```
<JumboTronComponent>
      This is a long sentence, and I want to insert content into the
      jumbotron component from the outside.
</JumboTronComponent>
```

That is to say, we want to insert content into the jumbotron component from the outside. To do so, we use *this.props.children* as shown below:

```
import React, { Component } from 'react';
import { Jumbotron, Button } from 'react-bootstrap';

class JumboTronComponent extends Component {

  constructor(props){
    super(props);
  }
```

```
  render() {
    return (
      <div>
        <Jumbotron>
            <h1>Hello, world!</h1>
            <p>{this.props.children}</p>
            <p><Button variant="primary">Learn more</Button></p>
        </Jumbotron>
      </div>
    );
  }
}

export default JumboTronComponent;
```

If there is a string in between an opening and closing tag, the string is passed as a special prop: *props.children*. So, in the code above, *this.props.children* will be the string between *<JumboTronComponent>* and *</JumboTronComponent>* as shown in **bold** below:

```
<JumboTronComponent>
        This is a long sentence, and I want to insert content into the
        jumbotron component from the outside.
</JumboTronComponent>
```

*Summary*

In this chapter, we introduced the inline if '&&' operator that gives us more conditional control in rendering our JSX. We have also learned about inserting content into components from the outside using *props.children*.

Contact me at support@i-ducate.com if you encounter any issues or visit my GitHub repository at https://github.com/greglim81/react-chapter5 for the source code of Product.js and JumboTronComponent.js.

# CHAPTER 6: BUILDING FORMS USING FORMIK

In this chapter, we look at how to implement forms in React using an external library called Formik. Why use an external library to create Forms you might ask? You can certainly create Forms in React without an external library but as requirements for the Form increase for example, validation of form fields, you will realize (annoyingly) that one has to create a lot of code to get values in and out of the form state, validation and showing of error messages and handling form submissions. This leads to unorganized code and unnecessary complexity. You can see an example of such a form in https://github.com/greglim81/react-chapter6/blob/master/src/old-UserForm.js. This is actually the old form code for this chapter.

Using Formik (https://jaredpalmer.com/formik/), it helps us with these annoying parts and keeps code organized. Install Formik with the following command:

```
npm install formik --save
```

## 6.1 Create an Initial Form Template

First, either in a new React project or in your existing project from chapter 5, create a new file UserForm.js and copy and paste the form template from the Formik Overview site under "Reducing boilerplate" (https://jaredpalmer.com/formik/docs/overview).

**Getting Started**

Overview

Tutorial

Resources

**Guides**

Validation

Arrays and Nested Objects

TypeScript

React Native

Form Submission

**API Reference**

<Formik />

withFormik()

<FieldArray />

<Form />

**Reducing boilerplate**

The code above is very explicit about exactly what Formik is doing. `onChange` -> `handleChange` , `onBlur` -> `handleBlur` , and so on. However, to save you time, Formik comes with a few extra components to make life easier and less verbose: `<Form />` , `<Field />` , and `<ErrorMessage />` . They use React context to hook into the parent `<Formik />` state/methods.

```
// Render Prop
import React from 'react';
import { Formik, Form, Field, ErrorMessage } from 'formik';

const Basic = () => (
  <div>
    <h1>Any place in your app!</h1>
    <Formik
      initialValues={{ email: '', password: '' }}
      validate={values => {
        let errors = {};
        if (!values.email) {
          errors.email = 'Required';
        } else if (
          !/^[A-Z0-9._%+-]+@[A-Z0-9.-]+\.[A-Z]{2,}$/i.test(values.email)
        ) {
          errors.email = 'Invalid email address';
        }
```

🗎 Copy

Your UserForm.js should look like the below (note that I have modified it slightly for ES6):

```
import React, { Component } from 'react';
import { Formik, Form, Field, ErrorMessage } from 'formik';

class UserForm extends Component {
  constructor(props){
    super(props);
  }

  render(){
    return(
      <div>
          <h1>Any place in your app!</h1>
          <Formik
            initialValues={{ email: '', password: '' }}
            validate={values => {
              let errors = {};
              if (!values.email) {
                errors.email = 'Required';
              } else if (
                !/^[A-Z0-9._%+-]+@[A-Z0-9.-]+\.[A-
Z]{2,}$/i.test(values.email)
                ) {
                errors.email = 'Invalid email address';
              }
              return errors;
            }}
            onSubmit={(values, { setSubmitting }) => {
              setTimeout(() => {
                alert(JSON.stringify(values, null, 2));
                setSubmitting(false);
              }, 400);
            }}
          >
            {({ isSubmitting }) => (
              <Form>
                <Field type="email" name="email" />
                <ErrorMessage name="email" component="div" />
                <Field type="password" name="password" />
                <ErrorMessage name="password" component="div" />
                <button type="submit" disabled={isSubmitting}>
                  Submit
                </button>
              </Form>
            )}
          </Formik>
```

```
            </div>
        )
    }
}

export default UserForm;
```

If you run your code (do remember to initialize the UserForm component in App.js), you should have the form appearing. Try entering values into the form and when you click submit, there will be a popup with the values in a JSON object.

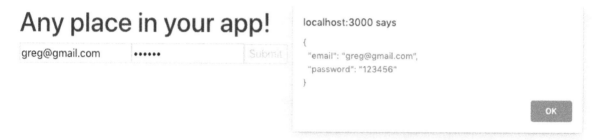

## Code Explanation

```
import React, { Component } from 'react';
import { Formik, Form, Field, ErrorMessage } from 'formik';
```

First, we import the necessary Formik components that will be used.

```
<Formik
        initialValues={{ email: '', password: '' }}
```

Next, we have the <Formik /> component with its *initialValues* attribute. *initialValues* as its name suggest populates the initial field values of the form. It also makes these values available to the *render* method as *values* i.e. *values.email* and *values.password*.

```
        validate={values => {
          let errors = {};
          if (!values.email) {
            errors.email = 'Required';
          } else if (
            !/^[A-Z0-9._%+-]+@[A-Z0-9.-]+\.[A-
Z]{2,}$/i.test(values.email)
          ) {
            errors.email = 'Invalid email address';
          }
          return errors;
```

```
      }}
```

We then have the *validate* function to validate the form's *values*. We first initialize an empty *errors* object to store the error message(s). We first check if the email field is empty using `if (!values.email)`. If so, assign *errors.email* to be 'Required'. Next, we check if the email is a valid email address using the expression: *if (!/^[A-Z0-9._%+-]+@[A-Z0-9.-]+\.[A-Z]{2,}$/i.test(values.email)).*

```
onSubmit={(values, { setSubmitting }) => {
  setTimeout(() => {
    alert(JSON.stringify(values, null, 2));
    setSubmitting(false);
  }, 400);
}}
>
```

We then have our *onSubmit* form submission handler. We pass in the form's *values* and a promise which shows an alert box with the submitted form values in a JSON object.

```
{({ isSubmitting }) => (
  <Form>
    <Field type="email" name="email" />
    <ErrorMessage name="email" component="div" />
    <Field type="password" name="password" />
    <ErrorMessage name="password" component="div" />
    <button type="submit" disabled={isSubmitting}>
      Submit
    </button>
  </Form>
)}
```

The body of the Form is created with the <Form /> component which is a small wrapper around the HTML <form> element. In the <Form /> we have the <Field /> component which hook up inputs to Formik. It uses the *name* attribute to match up with the Formik state (i.e. *values.email*, *values.password*). <Field /> defaults to an HTML <input /> element.

Below each <Field />, we have an <ErrorMessage /> component. <ErrorMessage /> renders the error message of a given field that has been visited. It is important that a field is visited first before we show any errors as we should avoid showing errors prematurely before the user has had a chance to edit the value, for example when the form is freshly loaded.

When you run your form, try placing your cursor in the email field and then moving away from it. You will see the validation error message 'Required' appearing.

56

# Any place in your app!

Required

Submit

Likewise, when you fill in an invalid email address, the validation error message 'invalid email address' appears.

# Any place in your app!

greglim.com

Invalid email address

Submit

We can easily include other custom validation like email, password minimum length. We will implement this in the next section.

## 6.2 Adding more Custom Validation

To add a custom validation to check for email and password minimum length, add the below codes in bold:

```
        ...
    <Formik
      initialValues={{ email: '', password: '' }}
      validate={values => {
        let errors = {};
        if (!values.email) {
          errors.email = 'Required';
        } else if (
          !/^[A-Z0-9._%+-]+@[A-Z0-9.-]+\.[A-
Z]{2,}$/i.test(values.email)
        ) {
          errors.email = 'Invalid email address';
        }
        else if (values.email.length < 10) {
          errors.email = 'Email address too short';
        }
```

```
    if (!values.password) {
      errors.password = 'Required';
    }
    else if (values.password.length < 8) {
      errors.password = 'Password too short';
    }
    return errors;
  }}
  ...
```

*Code Explanation*

```
    else if (values.email.length < 10) {
      errors.email = 'Email address too short';
    }
```

Here, we check if the email length is less than 10, following which we assign *errors.email* with the appropriate error message. We do a similar validation for the password field with the below code:

```
    if (!values.password) {
      errors.password = 'Required';
    }
    else if (values.password.length < 8) {
      errors.password = 'Password too short';
    }
```

## 6.3 Formatting Validation Error Messages

Our error messages are currently however not very prominent.

# Any place in your app!

greglim.com

Invalid email address

Submit

It would be better if we change the error messages' font color to red and to bold it. We do so by adding a *span* tag to it:

```
    {(({ isSubmitting }) => (
```

58

```
          <Form>
            <Field type="email" name="email" />
            <span style={{ color:"red", fontWeight: "bold" }}>
              <ErrorMessage name="email" component="div" />
            </span>
            <Field type="password" name="password" />
            <span style={{ color:"red", fontWeight: "bold" }}>
              <ErrorMessage name="password" component="div" />
            </span>
            <button type="submit" disabled={isSubmitting}>
              Submit
            </button>
          </Form>
        )}
```

Now our error messages appear more prominently:

# Any place in your app!

g@mail.c

Invalid email address

•••

Password too short

Submit

Below lists the complete code for UserForm.js which is also available in my React GitHub repository (https://github.com/greglim81/react-chapter6).

```
import React, { Component } from 'react';
import { Formik, Form, Field, ErrorMessage } from 'formik';

class UserForm extends Component {
  constructor(props){
    super(props);
  }

  render(){
    return(
      <div>
          <h1>Any place in your app!</h1>
          <Formik
            initialValues={{ email: '', password: '' }}
```

```
    validate={values => {
      let errors = {};
      if (!values.email) {
        errors.email = 'Required';
      } else if (
        !/^[A-Z0-9._%+-]+@[A-Z0-9.-]+\.[A-Z]{2,}$/i.test(values.email)
      ) {
        errors.email = 'Invalid email address';
      }
      else if (values.email.length < 10) {
        errors.email = 'Email address too short';
      }

      if (!values.password) {
        errors.password = 'Required';
      }
      else if (values.password.length < 8) {
        errors.password = 'Password too short';
      }
      return errors;
    }}
    onSubmit={(values, { setSubmitting }) => {
      setTimeout(() => {
        alert(JSON.stringify(values, null, 2));
        setSubmitting(false);
      }, 400);
    }}
  >
    {({ isSubmitting }) => (
      <Form>
        <Field type="email" name="email" />
        <span style={{ color:"red", fontWeight: "bold" }}>
          <ErrorMessage name="email" component="div" />
        </span>
        <Field type="password" name="password" />
        <span style={{ color:"red", fontWeight: "bold" }}>
          <ErrorMessage name="password" component="div" />
        </span>
        <button type="submit" disabled={isSubmitting}>
          Submit
        </button>
      </Form>
    )}
  </Formik>
</div>
```

```
      )
    }
}
```

```
export default UserForm;
```

*Summary*

In this chapter, we learned how to create a form using the Formik library. We learned how to handle form inputs, show specific form field validation errors and perform form submission.

Now after submitting a form, we need to persist the data by calling the API endpoint of the server. We will begin to explore how to communicate with the server in the next chapter.

# CHAPTER 7: GETTING DATA FROM RESTFUL APIS WITH AXIOS

In this chapter, we will see how to call backend services to get data through RESTful APIs with the Axios library.

## 7.1 GitHub RESTful API

Building RESTful APIs is beyond the scope of React because React is a client-side technology whereas building RESTful APIs require server-side technology like NodeJS, ASP.NET, Ruby on Rails and so on. (Later on in chapter 9, we will introduce Firebase, which provides us with a simple way for us to create and store server-side data that we can utilize to build a fully functioning React application!)

We will illustrate by connecting to the GitHub RESTful API to retrieve and manage GitHub content. You can know more about the GitHub API at

```
https://developer.github.com/v3/
```

But as a quick introduction, we can get GitHub users data with the following url,

```
https://api.github.com/search/users?q=<search term>
```

We simply specify our search term in the url to get GitHub data for user with name matching our search term. An example is shown below with search term *greg*.

```
https://api.github.com/search/users?q=greg
```

When we make a call to this url, we will get the following json objects as a result (fig. 7.1.1).

```
← → C ⟲ ⌂    🔒 Secure  https://api.github.com/search/users?q=greg
```

```
{
  "total_count": 14813,
  "incomplete_results": false,
  "items": [
    {
      "login": "gregkh",
      "id": 14953,
      "avatar_url": "https://avatars0.githubusercontent.com/u/14953?v=3",
      "gravatar_id": "",
      "url": "https://api.github.com/users/gregkh",
      "html_url": "https://github.com/gregkh",
      "followers_url": "https://api.github.com/users/gregkh/followers",
      "following_url": "https://api.github.com/users/gregkh/following{/other_user}",
      "gists_url": "https://api.github.com/users/gregkh/gists{/gist_id}",
      "starred_url": "https://api.github.com/users/gregkh/starred{/owner}{/repo}",
      "subscriptions_url": "https://api.github.com/users/gregkh/subscriptions",
      "organizations_url": "https://api.github.com/users/gregkh/orgs",
      "repos_url": "https://api.github.com/users/gregkh/repos",
      "events_url": "https://api.github.com/users/gregkh/events{/privacy}",
      "received_events_url": "https://api.github.com/users/gregkh/received_events",
      "type": "User",
      "site_admin": false,
      "score": 45.86066
    },
    {
      "login": "greg",
      "id": 1658846,
      "avatar_url": "https://avatars0.githubusercontent.com/u/1658846?v=3",
      "gravatar_id": "",
      "url": "https://api.github.com/users/greg",
      "html_url": "https://github.com/greg",
      "followers_url": "https://api.github.com/users/greg/followers",
      "following_url": "https://api.github.com/users/greg/following{/other_user}",
      "gists_url": "https://api.github.com/users/greg/gists{/gist_id}",
      "starred_url": "https://api.github.com/users/greg/starred{/owner}{/repo}",
      "subscriptions_url": "https://api.github.com/users/greg/subscriptions",
      "organizations_url": "https://api.github.com/users/greg/orgs",
      "repos_url": "https://api.github.com/users/greg/repos",
      "events_url": "https://api.github.com/users/greg/events{/privacy}",
      "received_events_url": "https://api.github.com/users/greg/received_events",
      "type": "User",
      "site_admin": false,
      "score": 44.028103
    },
```

fig. 7.1.1

## 7.2 Getting Data

To get data using a RESTful API, we are going to use the Axios library. Axios is a promise-based http client for the browser and Node.js. We use it to make ajax calls to the server.

Axios provides the *get()* method for getting a resource, *post()* for creating it, *put()* for updating it, *delete()* for delete and *head()* for getting metadata regarding a resource. We will illustrate using Axios to get data from a RESTful API in the following code example.

To begin, either create a new React project or in your existing project from chapter 6, in *src* folder, create a new file GitHub.js with the below code.

```
import React, { Component } from 'react';
import axios from 'axios'; // npm install axios

class GitHub extends Component {

    constructor(){
        super();
        this.getGitHubData('greg');
    }

    getGitHubData(_searchTerm){
        axios.get("https://api.github.com/search/users?q="+_searchTerm)
            .then(res => {
                console.log(res.data.items);
            });
    }

    render() {
        return (
          <div>
          </div>
        );
    }
}
export default GitHub;
```

*getGitHubData* is a method that will return GitHub data from our API endpoint. To call our API endpoint, we need to use the *axios* library. First, install *axios* by executing the following in Terminal:

```
npm install axios
```

Then in GitHub.js, import it using

```
import axios from 'axios';
```

In the constructor, we call the *getGitHubData* method with argument 'greg'. The *getGitHubData* method returns a Promise which we need to subscribe to.

```
getGitHubData(_searchTerm){
    axios.get("https://api.github.com/search/users?q="+_searchTerm)
        .then(res => {
            console.log(res.data.items);
        });
}
```

Note: If you are unfamiliar with promises, a promise allows us to make sense out of asynchronous behavior. Promises provide handlers with an asynchronous action's eventual success value. Initially, the promise is pending, and then it can either be fulfilled with a value or be rejected with an error reason. When either of these options happens, the associated handlers queued up by a promise's then method are called. This lets asynchronous methods return values like synchronous methods instead of immediately returning the final value. The asynchronous method returns a promise to supply the value at some point in the future.

In *getGitHubData*, we use the *get()* method of *axios* and give the url of our API endpoint. We have a search term provided by the user from an input which we will implement later. The return type of *get()* is an promise. We subscribe to this promise with *then* so that when an ajax call is completed, the response is fed to the Promise and then pushed to the component.

We then pass in our callback function *res => console.log(res.data.items)*. Note that we have to access *data.items* property to get the *items* array direct as that is the json structure of the GitHub response. So when our ajax call is completed, we print the list of items returned which is the GitHub users search results.

*Running our App*

Before we run our app, remember that we have to import and call our GitHub component in App.js.

```
import React, { Component } from 'react';
import GitHub from './GitHub';

class App extends Component {

  render() {
    return (
      <div>
        <GitHub />
      </div>
    );
  }
}

export default App;
```

Now run your app in Chrome. Go to 'View', 'Developer', 'Developer Tools'. Under console, you can see the following result from the console (fig. 7.2.1). The

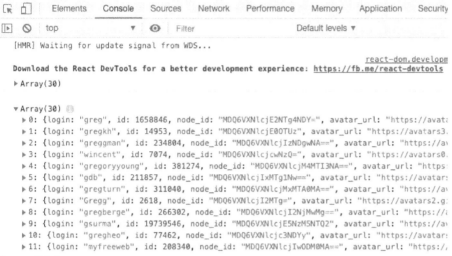

figure 7.2.1

Our requested json object is a single object containing an items array of size 30 with each item representing the data of a GitHub user.

Each *user* object has properties *avatar_url*, *html_url*, *login*, *score*, and so on (fig. 7.2.2).

▼Array(30)
  ▼0:
      login: "greg"
      id: 1658846
      node_id: "MDQ6VXNlcjE2NTg4NDY="
      avatar_url: "https://avatars3.githubusercontent.com/u/1658846?v=4"
      gravatar_id: ""
      url: "https://api.github.com/users/greg"
      html_url: "https://github.com/greg"
      followers_url: "https://api.github.com/users/greg/followers"
      following_url: "https://api.github.com/users/greg/following{/other_user}"
      gists_url: "https://api.github.com/users/greg/gists{/gist_id}"
      starred_url: "https://api.github.com/users/greg/starred{/owner}{/repo}"
      subscriptions_url: "https://api.github.com/users/greg/subscriptions"
      organizations_url: "https://api.github.com/users/greg/orgs"
      repos_url: "https://api.github.com/users/greg/repos"
      events_url: "https://api.github.com/users/greg/events{/privacy}"
      received_events_url: "https://api.github.com/users/greg/received_events"

figure 7.2.2

## 7.3 Life Cycle *componentDidMount*

Even though our code currently works, it doesn't follow best practices. We are currently calling the server in the constructor of the app component. As a best practice, constructors should be lightweight and should not contain any costly operations making it easier to test and debug. So where should we move our code to?

Components have a lifecycle which is managed by React. There are lifecycle hooks which we can tap into when a component is mounted or updated. These methods are invoked either before or after the component renders the UI. To do this, we need to implement one or more of the following interfaces in the component.

*constructor(props)*
*render()*
*componentDidMount()*

Note: The constructor is not technically a lifecycle method, but we include it as it is called when a component first initializes. The constructor is also where we should initialize the state since it is always the first function invoked when a component is mounted. For completeness sake, I also mention the *componentWillMount()* life cycle method which is called before any HTML element is rendered. But *constructor* already allows to execute code before *render*. Therefore, you can safely ignore the *componentWillMount()* life cycle method.

Each of the interfaces has a method that we can implement in our component. When the right moment arrives, React will call these methods. In the following, we will implement the *componentDidMount()* interface which is notified after the first render of the component. This is where ajax requests and DOM or state updates should occur.

In terms of lifecycle, *componentDidMount()* is called after the constructor. So in the constructor, we do lightweight and basic initialization and if we need to call the server, we do it in *componentDidMount*. So we shift the code to call GitHub from the constructor to *componentDidMount* as shown below.

```
class GitHub extends Component {

    constructor(){
        super();
    }

    componentDidMount(){
        this.getGitHubData('greg');
    }

    getGitHubData(_searchTerm){
```

```
            axios.get("https://api.github.com/search/users?q="+_searchTerm)
                .then(res => {
                    console.log(res.data.items);
                });
    }
```

## 7.4 Showing a Loader Icon

While getting content from a server, it is often useful to show a loading icon to the user (fig. 7.4.1).

figure 7.4.1

To do so, in app component, create a state variable called *isLoading* and set it to *true* like in the below code.

```
class GitHub extends Component {

    constructor(){
        super();
        this.state = {
            isLoading : true
        };
    }
```

*isLoading* will be true when loading of results from server is still going on. We set it to true in the beginning since we call *getGitHubData* in *componentDidMount*.

Next, in the *then()* method, set *isLoading* to false because at this point, we get the results from the server and loading is finished.

```
    getGitHubData(_searchTerm){
        axios.get("https://api.github.com/search/users?q="+_searchTerm)
            .then(res => {
                this.setState({
                    isLoading : false,
                })
                console.log(res.data.items);
            });
    }
```

Lastly, in *render()*, add a *div* that shows the loading icon. We use the if @@ conditional to make the *div* visible only when the component is loading.

```
render() {
 return (
   <div>
      { this.state.isLoading &&
           <h4>Getting data...</h4>
      }
   </div>
 );
```

If you load your app in the browser, you should see the "Getting data" message being displayed for a short moment before data from the server is loaded.

We will now replace the "Getting data" message with the loading icon. To get the loading icon, go to https://www.npmjs.com/package/react-loading. *React-loading* is a library that provides many easy to use animations for React projects (fig. 7.4.2).

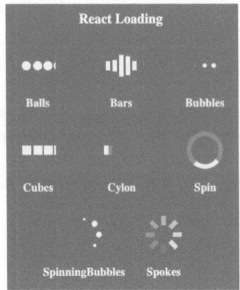

figure 7.4.2

Install the *react-loading* library in the Terminal with the code:

```
npm install react-loading
```

Back in GitHub.js, import *ReactLoading* with the statement:

```
import ReactLoading from 'react-loading';
```

To add the loading icon, replace the *"Getting data..."* message with the following code in bold:

```
<div>
  { this.state.isLoading &&
      <ReactLoading type="spinningBubbles" color="#444" />
  }
</div>
```

We use the *<ReactLoading>* tag and specify *spinningBubbles* as the type to render the spinning bubbles animation. You can try out other kinds of animations as specified in the *react-loading* documentation.

## 7.5 Implementing a GitHub Results Display Page

We will now implement a page which displays our GitHub user data nicely like in figure 7.5.1.

# GitHub Users Results

 Login: greg
Id: 1658846

 Login: gregkh
Id: 14953

 Login: greggman
Id: 234804

 Login: gregoryyoung
Id: 381274

 Login: wincent
Id: 7074

figure 7.5.1

First, we need to declare and initialize an empty *data* array in our state. We declare it in our constructor as *data : []* as shown below.

```
constructor(){
    super();
    this.state = {
```

```
        data: [],
        isLoading : true
    };
}
```

We then subscribe to our promise returned from *getGitHubData* and assign the returned result to *data* array. Note once again that we assign it with *data.items* as this is the users *item* array structured in the json response.

```
getGitHubData(_searchTerm){
    axios.get("https://api.github.com/search/users?q="+_searchTerm)
        .then(res => {
            this.setState({
                isLoading : false,
                data: res.data.items
            })
        });
}
```

Next, we want to render our GitHub user data nicely. In *render()*, we use the react-bootstrap *Media Object* component from *https://react-bootstrap.github.io/layout/media/* as what we have done previously.

We will slightly modify the markup from *getbootstrap* and include it in our component as shown below:

```
render() {
    const listUsers = this.state.data.map((user) =>
        <Media key={user.id}>
            <a href={user.html_url}>
                <img
                    width={64}
                    height={64}
                    className="mr-3"
                    src={user.avatar_url}
                    alt="Generic placeholder"
                />
            </a>
            <Media.Body>
                <h5>Login: {user.login}</h5>
                <p>Id: { user.id }</p>
            </Media.Body>
        </Media>
    );

    return (
```

```
    <div>
       <h3>GitHub Users Results</h3>
       { this.state.isLoading &&
            <ReactLoading type="spinningBubbles" color="#444" />
       }
       {listUsers}
    </div>
  );
}
```

Lastly, import the elements used in the react-bootstrap component with the import statement. Remember to install react-bootstrap if you have not done so.

```
import { Media, Form, FormGroup, FormControl, Button } from 'react-
bootstrap';
```

*Code Explanation*

```
const listUsers = this.state.data.map((user) => <Media>…
```

We use *map* to repeat the media object for each user data we get from GitHub.

We then add Javascript JSX expressions wrapped in {} inside the template. The user's id, html_url, avatar_url and login.

```
<Media key={user.id}>
    <a href={user.html_url}>
        <img
            width={64}
            height={64}
            className="mr-3"
            src={user.avatar_url}
            alt="Generic placeholder"
        />
    </a>
    <Media.Body>
        <h5>Login: {user.login}</h5>
        <p>Id: { user.id }</p>
    </Media.Body>
</Media>
```

Finally, we display our data by including *listUsers* in our return template as shown below:

```
return (
  <div>
    <h3>GitHub Users Results</h3>
    { this.state.isLoading &&
        <ReactLoading type="spinningBubbles" color="#444" />
    }
    {listUsers}
  </div>
);
```

If you run your app now, you should get a similar page as shown below.

## GitHub Users Results

 Login: greg
Id: 1658846

 Login: gregkh
Id: 14953

 Login: greggman
Id: 234804

 Login: gregoryyoung
Id: 381274

 Login: wincent
Id: 7074

## 7.6 Adding an Input to GitHub Results Display Page

We are currently hard-coding our search term to '*greg*' in our request to GitHub. We will now use a search input so that a user can type in her search terms and retrieve the relevant search result.

The final GitHub component code will look like below. The first change is that we will not make a call to GitHub through *componentDidMount* in the beginning as we will make the call only when a user clicks on Submit. Therefore, we can remove *componentDidMount*

Next, in the constructor, we initialize *isLoading* to *false* at first since no call to GitHub is made at the beginning. We add a state property '*searchTerm*' which will be entered by the user. We also add the bindings for the *handleChange* and *handleSubmit* methods of the form.

```
constructor(){
    super();
```

74

```
this.state = {
    data: [],
    searchTerm:'',
    isLoading : false
};

this.handleChange = this.handleChange.bind(this);
this.handleSubmit = this.handleSubmit.bind(this);
}
```

Once the user submits the form, we set *isLoading* to *true* just before the call to *getGitHubData* to show the loading icon.

```
handleSubmit(e) {
    e.preventDefault();
    this.setState({
        isLoading : true
    })
    this.getGitHubData(this.state.searchTerm);
}
```

Once we get notified of results from our GitHub request, we set *isLoading* to *false* in *getGitHubData* to hide the loading icon.

```
getGitHubData(_searchTerm){
    axios.get("https://api.github.com/search/users?q="+_searchTerm)
        .then(res => {
            this.setState({
                isLoading : false,
                data: res.data.items
            })
            console.log(res.data.items);
        });
}
```

Next, add the *<Form>* component as shown in **bold**:

```
return (
  <div>
    <Form inline onSubmit={this.handleSubmit}>
      <Form.Group controlId="formInlineName">
        <Form.Control
            type="text"
            value={this.state.searchTerm}
            placeholder="Enter Search Term"
```

```
            onChange={this.handleChange}
        />
    </Form.Group>
    {' '}
    <Button type="submit">
        Search
    </Button>
</Form>
<h3>GitHub Users Results</h3>
{ this.state.isLoading &&
    <ReactLoading type="spinningBubbles" color="#444" />
}
{listUsers}
</div>
);
```

Also import the *Form* and *Button* components from react-bootstrap:

```
import { Media, Form, Button } from 'react-bootstrap';
```

We use the Form inline to render a simple form with a single input (fig. 7.6.1) which is binded to the state's *searchTerm* property.

figure 7.6.1

Remember to implement the *handleChange* method which sets the keyed input to the state.

```
handleChange(e) {
    this.setState({ searchTerm: e.target.value });
}
```

Also remove the call to *getGitHubData* in *componentDidMount*:

```
componentDidMount(){
    this.getGitHubData('greg');
}
```

*Running your App*

You can now see GitHub user results displayed as you submit your search terms.

## Summary

In the chapter, we learned how implement a GitHub User Search application by connecting our React app to the GitHub RESTful api using Axios, Promises, component lifecycles and displaying a loader icon.

# CHAPTER 8: ROUTING

We have so far covered displaying components in a single view. But what if we have multiple views that a user needs to navigate from one to the next? In this chapter, we will explore **Routers** that provide screen navigation in our React Single Page Application.

We are familiar with navigating websites. We enter a URL in the address bar and the browser navigates to a corresponding page. We click links on the page and the browser navigates to a new page. We click the browser's back and forward buttons and the browser navigates backward and forward through the history of pages we've seen.

The *React Router* library borrows from this model. It interprets a browser URL as an instruction to navigate to a client-generated view. It can also pass optional parameters along to the supporting view component to help it decide what specific content to present.

Note: React doesn't come with a standard router. *React Router* is a routing solution created by engineers Michael Jackson and Ryan Florence. It has been adopted by the React community as a popular solution for React apps.

We can bind the router to links on a page and it will navigate to the appropriate application view when the user clicks a link. We can also navigate imperatively when the user clicks a button, selects from a dropbox, or from other user-generated events. And because the router logs activity in the browser's history journal, the back and forward buttons work as well.

In this chapter, we will extend our project from chapter seven to add routing to navigate between Home, GitHub and Not Found components.

*Installing React-Routing-DOM*

The first step to building a Single Page application is to install the *react-router-dom* library by executing the below in the Terminal:

```
npm install --save react-router-dom
```

## 8.1 Setting Up Our Routes

After installing the *react-router-dom* library, we need to define our routes. Each route is an endpoint that can be entered into the browser's location bar. When a route is requested, we can render the appropriate content.

In your project from the previous chapter, add the following codes in App.js:

```
import React, { Component } from 'react';
import GitHub from './GitHub';
import {BrowserRouter, Route, Switch} from 'react-router-dom';

class App extends Component {
  render() {
    return (
      <div>
        <Header />
      </div>
    );
  }
}
export default App;

class Header extends Component {
  render(){
    return (
        <BrowserRouter>
          <div>
            <Switch>
              <Route path="/github" component={GitHub} />
              <Route exact path="/" component={Home} />
              <Route path="/*" component={NotFound} />
            </Switch>
          </div>
        </BrowserRouter>
    )
  }
}

class Home extends Component {
  render(){
    return (
      <div>
        Home
      </div>
    )
  }
}

class NotFound extends Component {
  render(){
```

```
      return <div>Not Found</div>
   }
}
```

*Code Explanation*

```
class App extends Component {
  render() {
    return (
      <div>
        <Header />
      </div>
    );
  }
}
```

First, in App, we render a Header component.

```
class Header extends Component {
  render(){
    return (
        <BrowserRouter>
          <div>
            <Switch>
              <Route path="/github" component={GitHub} />
              <Route exact path="/" component={Home} />
              <Route path="/*" component={NotFound} />
            </Switch>
          </div>
        </BrowserRouter>
    )
  }
}
```

Our header component contains *BrowserRouter*, *Switch* and *Route* imported from the 'react-router-dom' library which provide the essential routing functionalities.

*BrowserRouter* contains a list of *Route* components. The routes tell the router which component to render when the window's location changes. Each *Route* component associates a path to a component. Each *Route* definition has at least two properties, *path*, which is the unique name we assign to our route, and component which specifies the associated component. When the browser's location matches the path, the component will be displayed.

In our route definition, we have specified three components. GitHubComponent, HomeComponent, and NotFoundComponent. To make it easier to illustrate, we define HomeComponent and

81

NotFoundComponent in App.js instead of in separate files.

```
class Home extends Component {
  render(){
    return (
      <div>
        Home
      </div>
    )
  }
}

class NotFound extends Component {
  render(){
    return <div>Not Found</div>
  }
}
```

You will realize that HomeComponent and NotFoundComponent are very basic components that simply displays a message. This is to illustrate navigating to different views.

GitHub Component will simply contain the code we implemented back in chapter seven in App component.

```
<Route path="/github" component={GitHub} />
<Route exact path="/" component={Home} />
<Route path="/*" component={NotFound} />
```

Now, our route definition tells React that:

- if the path contains *'GitHub'*, React should create an instance of GitHubComponent and render it in the DOM.
- if the path contains '/', React should create an instance of HomeComponent and render it in the DOM. Notice that this route has the *exact* property. Why do we need *exact?* Without *exact*, routes are matched to a path *if the URL we are on **contains** the path.* This means that if someone navigates to '/github', because it contains '/', Home component will be shown as well. Thus, both GitHub and Home component will be shown at the same time which is not what we want. We therefore specify *exact* so that Home component will only be displayed when the location exactly matches the root '/'.
- Lastly, if a user navigates to a route that we have not defined, the path '/*' is a wildcard that catches all invalid routes and directs to NotFoundComponent.

In general, more specific route paths should be specified first, i.e. '/github'. Other more inclusive paths like '/*' should be specified later. An additional measure to avoid showing more than one component, is to wrap our routes within the *Switch* component.

```
<Switch>
  <Route path="/github" component={GitHub} />
  <Route exact path="/" component={Home} />
  <Route path="/*" component={NotFound} />
</Switch>
```

The *Switch* component only displays the first route that matches. This assures that only one of these routes will be rendered.

At this point, we can run the app and when you physically type the routes into the browser's location bar, you can watch the content change. We of course do not expect users to navigate our website by typing routes into the location bar. In the next section, we introduce the *Link* component provided by *react-router-dom* to create browser links.

## 8.2 Navigation Bar Links

*Links*

Having defined and configured our routes in Header component, we can now add our navigation links to Home and GitHub component. In App.js, add the below codes in bold.

```
...
import  {BrowserRouter,  Route,  Switch  }  from  'react-router-dom';
import { Nav, Navbar } from 'react-bootstrap';

...
class Header extends Component {
  render(){
    return (
        <BrowserRouter>
          <div>
            <Navbar bg="light" expand="lg">
              <Navbar.Brand href="#home">React-Bootstrap</Navbar.Brand>
              <Navbar.Toggle aria-controls="basic-navbar-nav" />
              <Navbar.Collapse id="basic-navbar-nav">
                <Nav className="mr-auto">
                  <Nav.Link href="/">Home</Nav.Link>
                  <Nav.Link href="/github">GitHub</Nav.Link>
                </Nav>
              </Navbar.Collapse>
            </Navbar>
```

```
      <Switch>
        <Route path="/github" component={GitHub} />
        <Route exact path="/" component={Home} />
        <Route path="/*" component={NotFound} />
      </Switch>
    </div>
  </BrowserRouter>
)
}
}
```

*Code Explanation*

The *Navbar* component markup (and along with its child components) is taken from react-bootstrap's navbar component template (https://react-bootstrap.github.io/components/navbar/). *Navbar* provides for a professional-looking navigation bar (fig. 8.2.1).

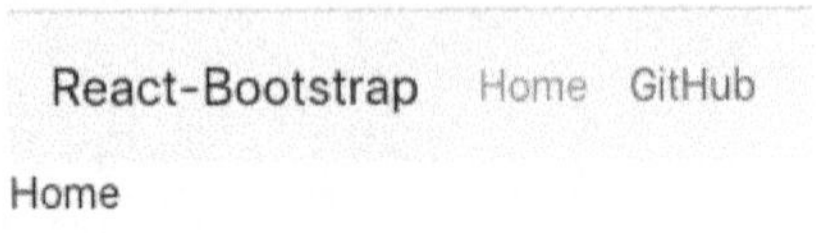

| React-Bootstrap | Home | GitHub |

Home

figure 8.2.1

Note that the default navbar in react-bootstrap renders a navbar with other items in it. We can get rid of the dropdown and keep only the Home and GitHub links for cleaner code.

```
          <Nav className="mr-auto">
            <Nav.Link href="/">Home</Nav.Link>
            <Nav.Link href="/github">GitHub</Nav.Link>
          </Nav>
```

We provide two navigation items in the navbar with two *NavItems*.

React Router will navigate the user to the target route specified by finding the route definition with that name. It will then create an instance of the component and render it

And if we try a non-existent route, we get a 'not found' page because we have earlier declared the wildcard path to direct to NotFoundComponent.

```
          <Switch>
            <Route path="/github" component={GitHub} />
            <Route exact path="/" component={Home} />
            <Route path="/*" component={NotFound} />
          </Switch>
```

84

If we run our app now, we'll get a view like in figure 8.2.2.

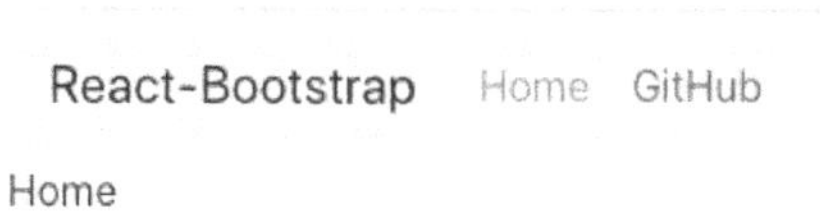

React-Bootstrap
Home
GitHub
Home

figure 8.2.2

And if we navigate to GitHub, we get the view like in figure 8.2.3

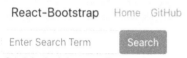

React-Bootstrap
Home
GitHub
Enter Search Term
Search
GitHub Users Results

figure 8.2.3

And when you try to enter in an unspecified url, you get the NotFoundComponent rendered like in figure 8.2.4

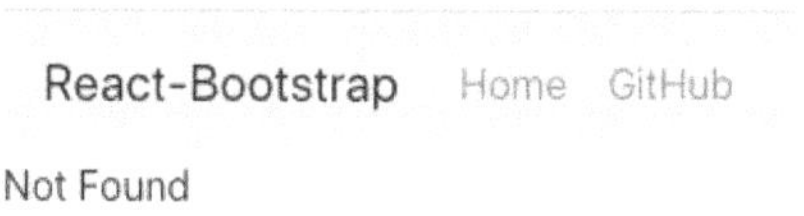

React-Bootstrap
Home
GitHub
Not Found

figure 8.2.4

## *Try It Yourself - Adding a New Link*

Now, try adding a new link on your own. Remember that you will have to add the new Link in the Header Component like below:

```
<Nav className="mr-auto">
  <Nav.Link href="/">Home</Nav.Link>
  <Nav.Link href="/github">GitHub</Nav.Link>
  <Nav.Link href="/<path_name>">Path Text</Nav.Link>
</Nav>
```

Next in Header, import the additional component and add the new path under *Switch* as shown below:

```
<Switch>
  <Route path="/github" component={GitHub} />
  <Route exact path="/" component={Home} />
  <Route exact path="<path_name>" component={YourOwnComponent} />
  <Route path="/*" component={NotFound} />
</Switch>
```

## 8.3 Route Parameters

We will now illustrate how to create routes that takes in route parameters. Why do we need this? For example, from the GitHub results page, if we want to navigate to a page to see the details of a specific GitHub user, we can pass in the information via route parameters.

In Header, we add a route that takes in two route parameters as shown below in **bold**.

```
...
import GitHubUser from './GitHubUser';
...

class Header extends Component {
  render(){
    return (
        <BrowserRouter>
          <div>
            <Navbar>
                    ...
            </Navbar>
            <Switch>
              <Route path="/github/user/:login/:id" component={GitHubUser} />
              <Route path="/github" component={GitHub} />
              <Route exact path="/" component={Home} />
              <Route path="/*" component={NotFound} />
            </Switch>
          </div>
        </BrowserRouter>
    )
  }
}
```

*Code Explanation*

We first import the GitHubUser component which we will implement later. The GitHubUser Component simply displays some information about a specific GitHub User.

Next, we add a route

```
<Route path="/github/user/:login/:id" component={GitHubUser} />
```

*/:login/:id* represents the *login* route parameter and the *id* route parameter. If we want to pass in only one parameter for e.g. *login*, it will be just *github/user/:login*. We can pass in multiple parameters (more than two) if we want to.

With this route, whenever we navigate to a url for e.g.

```
http://localhost:3000/GitHub/user/gregkh/45
```

React will render the GitHubUser Component with the parameter *login* 'gregkh' and *id* '45'.

You might ask, why is our route *github/user/:login/:id* and not *user/:login/:id*? That is because our GitHub search results is displayed in http://localhost:3000/GitHub/. If our search results is displayed in the root i.e. http://localhost:3000/, then our route will be *user/:login/:id*.

## Specifying Route Parameters

In this section, we illustrate specifying route parameters in each GitHubUser Link. In the template of GitHub.js, change the line in **bold**.

```
const listUsers = this.state.data.map((user) =>
            <Media key={user.id}>
                <Nav.Link href={`/github/user/${user.login}/${user.id}`}>
                    <img
                        width={64}
                        height={64}
                        className="mr-3"
                        src={user.avatar_url}
                        alt="Generic placeholder"
                    />
                </Nav.Link>
                <Media.Body>
                    <h5>Login: {user.login}</h5>
                    <p>Id: { user.id }</p>
                </Media.Body>
            </Media>
);
```

*Code Explanation*

```
<Nav.Link href={`/github/user/${user.login}/${user.id}`}>
```

```
<img
    width={64}
    height={64}
    className="mr-3"
    src={user.avatar_url}
    alt="Generic placeholder"
/>
</Nav.Link>
```

We add a *Nav.Link* to the user image of each search result. When one clicks on the user image, she will be routed to GitHubUser Component with parameters *login* and *id*. Note that ES6 allows us to use back ticks to bind our route parameters into the route path:

```
href={`/github/user/${user.login}/${user.id}`
```

## Retrieving Route Parameters

Next, we create GitHubUser Component that shows the details of a particular user. In our case, we will just show the login and id of the user. Create and fill in GitHubUser.js with the below code.

```
import React, { Component } from 'react';

class GitHubUser extends Component {

  constructor(props){
      super(props);
  }

  render() {
    return (
      <div>
        <h1>User Login: { this.props.match.params.login }</h1>
        <h2>User Id: { this.props.match.params.id }</h2>`
      </div>
    );
  }
}

export default GitHubUser;
```

*Code Explanation*

```
  render() {
    return (
```

```
     <div>
       <h1>User Login: { this.props.match.params.login }</h1>
       <h2>User Id: { this.props.match.params.id }</h2>`
     </div>
   );
 }
```

In the *render* method, we display *login* and *id* by getting the route parameters using:

```
       <h1>User Login: { this.props.match.params.login }</h1>
       <h2>User Id: { this.props.match.params.id }</h2>`
```

*this.props.match.params* is an object that holds all the values passed through parameters. We obtain the parameters by specifying them, in this case 'login' and 'id'.

*Running your App*

If you run your app now and click on one of the GitHub search results, you will be brought to the GitHubUser component which will show you the login and Id details of that GitHub user (fig. 10.3.1).

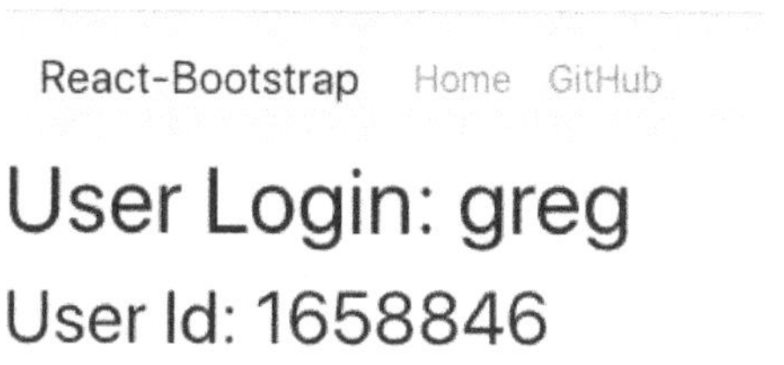

React-Bootstrap   Home   GitHub

# User Login: greg
## User Id: 1658846

`

figure 8.3.1

## 8.4 Programmatic Navigation

Suppose we want to redirect a user to another page upon clicking a button or upon clicking submit in a form. In such a case, we cannot use the *Nav.Link* directive. Instead, we need to talk to the React router directly and this is what we called programmatic navigation.

The below codes in GitHubUser.js illustrate this:

```
import React, { Component } from 'react';
import { Button } from 'react-bootstrap';

class GitHubUser extends Component {

  constructor(props){
```

```
      super(props);
      this.handleClick = this.handleClick.bind(this);
   }

   handleClick(e) {
      this.props.history.push("/github");
   }

   render() {
      return (
         <div>
            <h1>User Login: { this.props.match.params.login }</h1>
            <h2>User Id: { this.props.match.params.id }</h2>`
            <Button variant="primary" onClick={this.handleClick}>
               Go to GitHub Users
            </Button>
         </div>
      );
   }
}

export default GitHubUser;
```

*Code Explanation*

```
         <Button variant="primary" onClick={this.handleClick}>
            Go to GitHub Users
         </Button>
```

In *render*, we have a **Go to GitHub Users** button and we do event binding to bind it to the *handleClick()* method.

```
   constructor(props){
      super(props);
      this.handleClick = this.handleClick.bind(this);
   }
```

Remember to bind the method in the constructor:

```
   handleClick(e) {
      this.props.history.push("/github");
   }
```

In the *handleClick* method, we call the *push* method of *this.props.history* which takes in the name of the target route. When the user clicks on the button, the new route is pushed onto the *history* object. Pushing the route into *history* will cause the navigation to occur.

*Running your App*

If you run your app now, you will be able to go back to the GitHub page from the GitHubUsers page by clicking on the 'Go to GitHub Users' button.

## Summary

In this chapter, we learned how to build single page apps with routing. We learned how to define, configure and render requested components using the Route component. We also learned about providing route links, how to create routes with parameters and how to retrieve the parameters.

We have covered a lot in this chapter. Contact me at support@i-ducate.com if you have not already to have the full source code for this chapter or if you encounter any errors with your code.

# CHAPTER 9: C.R.U.D. WITH FIREBASE

In this chapter, we will cover how to implement full C.R.U.D. operations in React with a backend server. A typical web application architecture consists of the server side and client side. This book teaches you how to implement the client side using React. The client side talks to a backend server to get or save data via RESTful http services built using server-side frameworks like ASP.NET, Node.js and Ruby on Rails. We have explored this when we obtained data from the GitHub server in chapter seven.

Building the server side, however is often time-consuming and not within the scope of this course. In this chapter, however, we will explore using Firebase as our backend server. Firebase is Google's real-time database which offers a very powerful backend platform for building fast and scalable real-time apps.

With Firebase, we don't have to write server-side code or design relational databases. Firebase provides us with a real-time, fast and scalable NoSQL database in the cloud and we use a library to talk to this database. This allows us to focus on building our application according to requirements rather than debugging server-side code.

You might ask, what is a NoSQL database? In contrast to relational databases which consist of tables and relationships, in a NoSQL database, we have a tree of JSON objects and each node in the tree can have a different structure. Because we do not have to maintain table schemas, NoSQL databases provide us with one thing less to worry about, thereby increasing productivity. However, if your application involves lots of data aggregating, complex querying and reporting, a relational database might still be a better choice.

This chapter aims to illustrate create, read, update and delete functionality with React and Firebase integrated so that you can go on and create a fully working app. And if you choose to have a different backend server like ASP.NET, Node.js, the same principles will apply.

*More on Firebase*

Firebase is a real time database. which means that as data is modified, all connected clients are automatically refreshed in an optimized way. If one user adds a new item either through a browser or a mobile app, another user (again either through a browser or mobile app) sees the addition in real time without refreshing the page. Firebase of course provides more than just a real time database. It offers other services like Authentication, cloud messaging, disk space, hosting, analytics and more. You not only can develop React apps with Firestore as backend but also iOS, Android and web applications.

React and firebase work very well together especially in terms of receiving data and state management. This is because firebase provides real-time data synchronization by allowing us to subscribe to an event and give us a new set of data that we can readily call *setState* which re-renders our entire application.

## 9.1 Using Firebase

We can use Firebase features for free and only pay when our application grows bigger. You can choose between a subscription based or 'pay as you use' model. Find out more at firebase.google.com/pricing.

Before adding Firebase to our React project, we need to first create a Firebase account. Go to firebase.google.com and sign in with your Google account.

In the Firebase console (https://console.firebase.google.com/), click on 'Add Project' (figure 12.1)

figure 9.1.1

Fill in the project name, optionally enable Google Analytics for your project and click 'Create Project'.

When your project is created, in the project page, under "Get started by adding Firebase to your app', click on the </> icon to add firebase to our web app (figure 12.1.2).

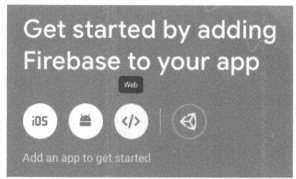

figure 9.1.2

Fill in a app nickname. Leave the Firebase Hosting checkbox unchecked for now since it can be setup later. Click 'Register app' (fig. 12.1.3).

×    Add Firebase to your web app

1    Register app

App nickname ⓘ

☐ Also set up **Firebase Hosting** for this app. Learn more ↗
Hosting can also be set up later. It's free to get started at any time.

Register app

2    Add Firebase SDK

figure 9.1.3

You will see some configuration code that you need to add in your project (fig. 9.1.4).

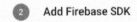

### Add Firebase SDK

Copy and paste these scripts into the bottom of your <body> tag, but before you use any Firebase services:

```html
<!-- The core Firebase JS SDK is always required and must be listed first -->
<script src="https://www.gstatic.com/firebasejs/7.13.2/firebase-app.js"></scrip

<!-- TODO: Add SDKs for Firebase products that you want to use
     https://firebase.google.com/docs/web/setup#available-libraries -->
<script src="https://www.gstatic.com/firebasejs/7.13.2/firebase-analytics.js"><

<script>
  // Your web app's Firebase configuration
  var firebaseConfig = {
    apiKey: "AIzaSyCOxp3etKT0NXT6TECx79EXQ6BorcBxXOM",
    authDomain: "angularcrud-b819e.firebaseapp.com",
    databaseURL: "https://angularcrud-b819e.firebaseio.com",
    projectId: "angularcrud-b819e",
    storageBucket: "angularcrud-b819e.appspot.com",
    messagingSenderId: "61064054237",
    appId: "1:61064054237:web:bd3bb5dd8cbf7599d1a234",
    measurementId: "G-2Y5SMQ4WL3"
  };
  // Initialize Firebase
  firebase.initializeApp(firebaseConfig);
  firebase.analytics();
</script>
```

figure 9.1.4

*Code Explanation*

```
<script src="https://www.gstatic.com/firebasejs/7.13.2/firebase-app.js"></script>
```

This is a script reference to Firebase SDK. firebase.js gives us a library to work with firebase.

```
<script>
  // Your web app's Firebase configuration
  var firebaseConfig = {
    apiKey: "AIzaSyCOxp3etKT0NXT6TECx79EXQ6BorcBxXOM",
    authDomain: "reactcrud-b819e.firebaseapp.com",
    databaseURL: "https://reactcrud-b819e.firebaseio.com",
    projectId: "reactcrud-b819e",
    storageBucket: "reactcrud-b819e.appspot.com",
```

96

```
  messagingSenderId: "61064054237",
  appId: "1:61064054237:web:bd3bb5dd8cbf7599d1a234",
  measurementId: "G-2Y5SMQ4WL3"
};
// Initialize Firebase
firebase.initializeApp(firebaseConfig);
firebase.analytics();
</script>
```

We have a *config* or configuration object with properties *apiKey*, *authDomain* (a subdomain under firebaseapp.com), *databaseUrl*, *storageBucket* (for storing files like photos, videos etc.), *messagingSenderId* (used for sending push notifications) and *appId*.

As instructed, copy and paste these scripts into the bottom of your <body> tag, but before you use any Firebase services.

## 9.2 Adding Firebase to our React App

To illustrate connecting Firebase to our React app, we will create a new project using create-react-app (I have named my project *ReactCRUD*). Remember to add react-bootstrap to your project.

```
create-react-app reactcrud
```

We will next use *npm* to add firebase to our project.

```
npm install firebase --save
```

*index.js*

In *index.js* of the newly created project, add the lines in **bold** below. Note that the credential properties in *firebaseConfig* should be your own (copied from firebase console)

```
import React from 'react';
import ReactDOM from 'react-dom';
import './index.css';
import App from './App';
import * as serviceWorker from './serviceWorker';
import * as firebase from 'firebase';

var config = {
    apiKey: "AIzaSyBN9WlmRc3SedmC4agM1G-rYqezGR22iZE",
    authDomain: "crudproject-45834.firebase       app.com",
    databaseURL: "https://crudproject-45834.firebaseio.com",
```

```
    projectId: "crudproject-45834",
    storageBucket: "crudproject-45834.appspot.com",
    messagingSenderId: "590481645308"
    appId: "..."
};

firebase.initializeApp(config);
ReactDOM.render(<App />, document.getElementById('root'));
serviceWorker.unregister();
```

We initialize firebase in our app with the configurations as provided in the firebase console. This lets us connect to the right database.

## *App.js*

Now to make sure that we have added firebase correctly to our project, go to App.js and add the lines **bold** below.

```
import React, { Component } from 'react';
import * as firebase from 'firebase';

class App extends Component {

  constructor(){
    super();
    console.log(firebase);
  }

  render() {
    return (
      <div>
        <h1></h1>
      </div>
    );
  }
}

export default App;
```

Make sure that the lite web server is running (by executing *npm start*) and in the console, you should see the firebase object printed in the console as shown in figure 9.2.1 to prove that we have added firebase correctly.

```
▼ {__esModule: true, initializeApp: f, app: f, registerVersion: f, setLogLevel: f, …}
  ▶ INTERNAL: {components: Map(26), registerComponent: f, removeApp: f, useAsService:
    SDK_VERSION: "7.14.1"
  ▶ User: f P(a, b, c)
  ▶ analytics: f (appArg)
  ▶ app: f app(name)
    apps: (...)
  ▶ auth: f (appArg)
  ▶ database: f (appArg)
  ▶ default: {__esModule: true, initializeApp: f, app: f, registerVersion: f, setLogLe
  ▶ firestore: f (appArg)
  ▶ functions: f (appArg)
  ▶ initializeApp: f ()
  ▶ installations: f (appArg)
  ▶ messaging: f (appArg)
  ▶ onLog: f onLog(logCallback, options)
  ▶ performance: f (appArg)
  ▶ registerVersion: f registerVersion(libraryKeyOrName, version, variant)
  ▶ remoteConfig: f (appArg)
```
figure 9.2.1

## 9.3 Working with a Firebase Database

Now let's look at our Firebase database. Go to console.firebase.google.com. Click on your project, and under 'Develop', click on **'Database'**. Under 'Realtime Database', click on **'Create database'** as shown in fig. 9.3.1.

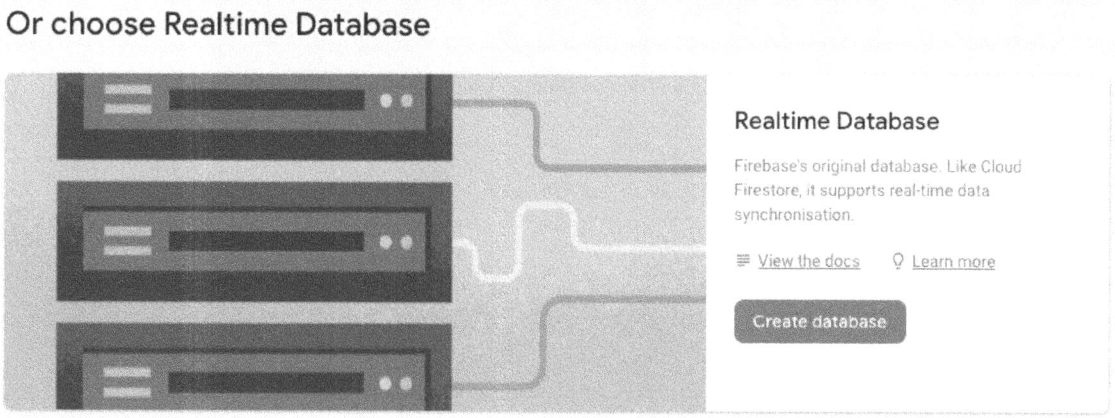

## Or choose Realtime Database

### Realtime Database

Firebase's original database. Like Cloud Firestore, it supports real-time data synchronisation.

≡ View the docs    ○ Learn more

Create database

Figure 9.3.1

On the next screen shown below (fig. 9.3.2), choose 'test mode' and then click 'Next'.

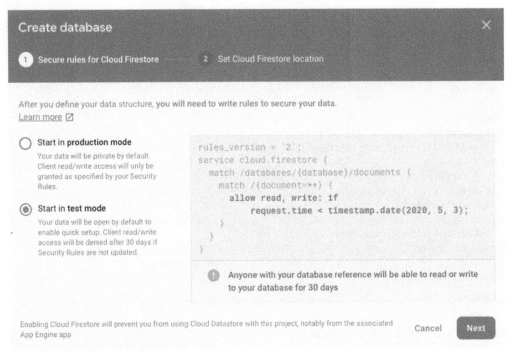

figure 9.3.2

Choose the default settings given for 'Cloud Firestore location' (fig. 9.3.3). It will then set up security rules.

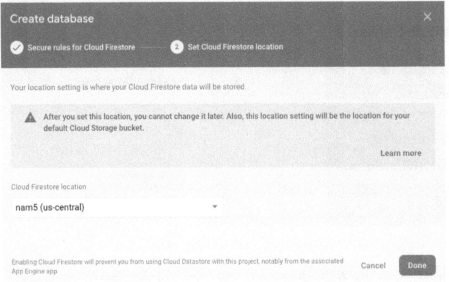

Figure 9.3.3

When you are brought back to the Database console, make sure that you select 'Realtime Database' and NOT 'Cloud Firestore' (fig. 9.3.4).

Figure 9.3.4

What's the difference between a Realtime Database and Cloud Firestore? To summarize, in Firestore, we store our data in terms of collections, and documents in these collections (fig. 12.3.5). But in a Realtime Database, we are essentially having a NoSQL database. In this chapter, we will be working with a Realtime database.

If you have not worked with NoSQL databases before, you might find it odd in the beginning because there is no concept of tables or relationships here. Our database is basically a tree of key value pair objects. We store json objects here that map natively to json objects in JavaScript. So when working with a NoSQL database on the backend, we get a json object from the server and we simply display in on the client. Or we construct a json object on the client and send it to server and we store it as it is. There is no additional mapping needed i.e. from relational format to json format or vice-versa.

Click + to add a new child node to the tree (fig. 9.3.5). Each node has a name and a value. Value can be a primitive type like string, boolean, number or it can be a complex object.

Figure 9.3.5

When you click **Add**, a new node will be added.

```
facedetector-246e5
  └── name: "Ervin Lim"
```

(Note that when you add a new child node, the child node gets highlighted in green and the parent node in yellow for a few seconds. If you try deleting a node, that node gets highlighted in red.)

Our values can also be complex objects. You can add complex objects by clicking on the + sign in `Value` of an existing child node. The below tree has a childnode 0 that contains further properties (fig. 9.3.6).

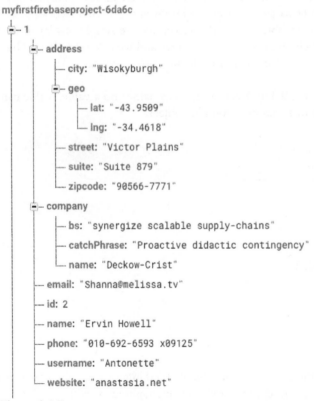

**crudproject-45834**

```
⊟ 0
    ┬── email: "Nathan@yesenia.net"
    ├── id: 3
    ├── name: "Clement Ong"
    └── username: "clem81"
 └── name: "Ervin Lim"
```

Figure 9.3.6

You can of course have complex objects in complex, for e.g. figure 9.3.7

**myfirstfirebaseproject-6da6c**

```
⊟ 1
  ⊟ address
      ┬── city: "Wisokyburgh"
      ├⊟ geo
      │    ┬── lat: "-43.9509"
      │    └── lng: "-34.4618"
      ├── street: "Victor Plains"
      ├── suite: "Suite 879"
      └── zipcode: "90566-7771"
  ⊟ company
      ┬── bs: "synergize scalable supply-chains"
      ├── catchPhrase: "Proactive didactic contingency"
      └── name: "Deckow-Crist"
  ── email: "Shanna@melissa.tv"
  ── id: 2
  ── name: "Ervin Howell"
  ── phone: "010-692-6593 x09125"
  ── username: "Antonette"
  └── website: "anastasia.net"
```

Figure 9.3.7

Essentially, we have a hierarchy of key value pairs in a NoSQL database. We don't have tables and relationships. The modeling of objects and their relationships vital to an enterprise level application is beyond the scope of this book.

In the next sections, we will illustrate with a simple example of user objects in our NoSQL database.

## 9.4 Displaying List of Users

We will illustrate how to display a list of users. But before that, we need to have existing user data in Firebase. We will use users data from jsonplaceholder at  http://jsonplaceholder.typicode.com/. jsonplaceholder provides with a fake online REST api and data for testing. So head to

http://jsonplaceholder.typicode.com/users

and save the json file. I have saved it as users.json. We can import this json file into our Firebase database by going to Database, click on the right most icon, and select 'Import JSON' (fig. 9.4.1).

figure 9.4.1

Browse to the user json file you saved and click 'Import' (fig. 9.4.2).

figure 9.4.2

103

The users data will be imported into firebase (fig. 9.4.3).

```
facedetector-246e5
 ⊟ 0
     ⊞ address
     ⊞ company
        email: "Sincere@april.biz"
        id: 1
        name: "Leanne Graham"
        phone: "1-770-736-8031 x56442"
        username: "Bret"
        website: "hildegard.org"
 ⊞ 1
 ⊞ 2
 ⊞ 3
```

figure 9.4.3

*User.js*

Next, we will create a user component to display our list of users. Create User.js in *src* with the following code.

```
import React, { Component } from 'react';
import * as firebase from 'firebase';

class User extends Component {

  constructor(props){
    super(props);
    this.state = {
        users: []
    };
  }

  componentDidMount(){
    firebase.database().ref('/')
      .on('value',snapshot => {
        console.log(snapshot.val())
      });
  }

  render() {
    return (
      <div>
```

```
      </div>
    );
  }
}

export default User;
```

*Code Explanation*

```
import * as firebase from 'firebase';
```

We import firebase and use it to access our database node in *componentDidMount*. Remember that *componentDidMount* is called after the first render of the component. This is where server requests and state updates should occur.

```
  componentDidMount(){
    firebase.database().ref('/')
      .on('value',snapshot => {
        console.log(snapshot.val())
      });
  }
```

In *componentDidMount*, we specify the location of a node in firebase as an argument to the *firebase.database().ref* method to retrieve our list of users. *firebase.database()* provides us with a Firebase Database service interface and its *ref* method returns the location in the Database corresponding to the provided path.

In our case, our list of users is at the root node and thus, we specify '/'. But say if our list of users is a child node under the parent node 'GitHub', we would then have something like

```
    firebase.database().ref('/GitHub')
```

We then listen for data changes at our specified location by providing a callback function to the *on* method:

```
componentDidMount(){
    firebase.database().ref('/')
      .on('value',snapshot => {
        console.log(snapshot.val())
      });
  }
```

This is the primary way to read data from a Database. Our callback will be triggered for the initial data and again whenever the data changes. That is, when we add, edit or delete a user, the callback will be triggered and we will have the updated list.

In the callback, we have a snapshot of *DataSnapshot* type that contains data from a Database location. Any time you read data from a firebase Database, you receive the data as a DataSnapshot. A DataSnapshot is passed to the event callback you attach with *on()*. You can extract the contents of the snapshot as a JavaScript object by calling the *val()* method.

In our case, `console.log(snapshot.val())` prints the contents of our snapshot as shown:

```
▼ {0: {…}, 1: {…}, 2: {…}, 3: {…}, 4: {…}, 5: {…}, 6: {…}, 7: {…}
  ▶ 0: {address: {…}, company: {…}, email: "Sincere@april.biz", ic
  ▶ 1: {address: {…}, company: {…}, email: "Shanna@melissa.tv", ic
  ▶ 2: {address: {…}, company: {…}, email: "Nathan@yesenia.net", i
  ▶ 3: {address: {…}, company: {…}, email: "Julianne.OConner@kory.
  ▶ 4: {address: {…}, company: {…}, email: "Lucio_Hettinger@annie.
  ▶ 5: {address: {…}, company: {…}, email: "Karley_Dach@jasper.inf
  ▶ 6: {address: {…}, company: {…}, email: "Telly.Hoeger@billy.biz
  ▶ 7: {address: {…}, company: {…}, email: "Sherwood@rosamond.me",
  ▶ 8: {address: {…}, company: {…}, email: "Chaim_McDermott@dana.i
```

If we run our app now, we can't see any data or will get an error saying something like "Permission denied. Client doesn't have permission to access the desired data." This is because in firebase, our firebase permission rules are currently configured as:

```
{
  "rules": {
    ".read": "auth != null",
    ".write": "auth != null"
  }
}
```

The above permissioning rule is a json object that determines the rules for reading and writing of data. You can access these rules in firebase console, under **Database**, **Rules** tab. Essentially, the code is saying that read and write permission is only granted to those who are logged in or authenticated *(auth != null)*. Because firebase authentication and authorization is beyond the scope of this book, and to quickly get a fully working React app, we will set both read and write permissions to be public, where anyone can read or write to our database.

So in firebase console in the Rules tab, edit the permission rules as shown below and click **Publish**. Note that whenever we make changes to our permission rules, we need to publish the changes.

```
{
  "rules": {
    ".read": true,
    ".write": true
  }
}
```

Now because Firebase is a NoSQL JSON data store, when we get some data from Firebase, we get an object containing keys and objects for all of our user data.

We will convert the returned single object to an array to help us iterate through the data easier by adding the codes in bold below:

```
componentDidMount(){
  firebase.database().ref('/')
    .on('value',snapshot => {
      let returnArr = [];
      snapshot.forEach(data => {
          var user = data.val();
          user['key'] = data.key;
          returnArr.push(user);
      });
      this.setState({
          users: returnArr
      })
    });
}
```

We declare an empty array *returnArr*, and for each object *data* in *snapshot*, we retrieve it with *data.val()*. We then assign the *key* property value to the *user* object. Remember that firebase generates and assigns a key value to an object that is newly added to the firebase database.

```
user['key'] = data.key;
```

The *key* property will be important for us later when we use it to retrieve a single specific object from firebase for deletion and update.

```
returnArr.push(user);
```

We then push it into *returnArr* and finally *setState returnArr* to *users*.

*User.js Render*

Now before we implement our template in *render()* of User.js, make sure that you have installed *react-bootstrap* with the following command in Terminal:

```
npm install --save react-bootstrap bootstrap
```

107

Make sure that you have also included the below css reference in index.js or App.js:

```
import 'bootstrap/dist/css/bootstrap.min.css';
```

Having done that, go to react-bootstrap website, and under 'Components', 'Tables' (https://react-bootstrap.github.io/components/table/), reference the *tables* code and in User.js, implement it in *render* like below:

```
render() {
  const listUsers = this.state.users.map((user) =>
  <tr key={user.key}>
    <td>{user.username}</td>
    <td>{user.email}</td>
    <td>Edit</td>
    <td>Remove</td>
  </tr>
  );

  return (
    <div>
      <Table striped bordered hover>
      <thead>
        <tr>
          <th>Username</th>
          <th>Email</th>
          <th>Edit</th>
          <th>Delete</th>
        </tr>
      </thead>
      <tbody>
        {listUsers}
      </tbody>
      </Table>
    </div>
  );
}
```

Remember to import *Table* with the import statement at the top:

```
import { Table } from 'react-bootstrap';
```

*Code Explanation*

```
<Table striped bordered condensed hover>
```

We use the bootstrap component *Table* to create a nice-looking table for listing our users (fig. 9.4.4).

| Username | Email | Edit | Delete |
|---|---|---|---|
| Antonettedfdssss | Shanna@melissa.tvdd | Edit | Remove |
| Samantha | Nathan@yesenia.net | Edit | Remove |
| Karianne223 | Julianne.OConner@kory.org23 | Edit | Remove |
| Kamren | Lucio_Hettinger@annie.ca | Edit | Remove |
| Elwyn.Skiles | Telly.Hoeger@billy.biz | Edit | Remove |
| Maxime_Nienow | Sherwood@rosamond.me | Edit | Remove |
| Delphine | Chaim_McDermott@dana.io | Edit | Remove |

figure 9.4.4

We also display *edit* and *remove* links in each row for the edit and delete operations we will implement later.

```
const listUsers = this.state.users.map((user) =>
<tr key={user.key}>
  <td>{user.username}</td>
  <td>{user.email}</td>
  <td>Edit</td>
  <td>Remove</td>
</tr>
);
```

# Preparing for Routing

In this section, we prepare to define our routes to our User component, a Not Found component and a User Form component for adding and editing users.

*App.js*

Create the routing configuration in App.js as shown below. Remember to run *npm install --save react-router-dom* if you have not already done so.

```
import React, { Component } from 'react';
import User from './User';
import {BrowserRouter, Route, Switch} from 'react-router-dom';
```

```
class App extends Component {

  render() {
    return (
      <div>
        <BrowserRouter>
          <div>
            <Switch>
              <Route exact path="/" component={User} />
              <Route path="/*" component={NotFound} />
            </Switch>
          </div>
        </BrowserRouter>
      </div>
    );
  }
}

export default App;

class NotFound extends Component {
  render() {
    return <div>Not Found</div>
  }
}
```

App.js currently contains two routes. The first is the exact path '/' which points to User component and the other is the wildcard path which points to NotFound component. We will extend the routes later to include the route to the User Add and Edit form. To make the code cleaner, we also removed the previous logging code to see if we have installed firebase correctly.

*Running your App*

Now if you run your app, you should see a list of users rendered.

Now, try going back to the firebase console and add a new user node. When you go back to your React app, you will realize that the user list is refreshed automatically with the new node! Or if you delete a node from the firebase console, the list is refreshed to reflect the deletion as well. And that'as the beauty of firebase. We achieved auto-refresh upon adding, updated, delete with the code we have implemented as shown below:

```
componentDidMount(){
  firebase.database().ref('/')
    .on('value',snapshot => {
```

```
        let returnArr = [];
        snapshot.forEach(data => {
            var user = data.val();
            user['key'] = data.key;
            returnArr.push(user);
        });
        this.setState({
            users: returnArr
        })
    });
}
```

## 9.5 Adding a User

*User.js*

Next, we will implement adding a user to our app by adding a button 'Add User' just before the user list in User.js. Add it and decorate it with bsStyle *primary* as shown in the code below:

```
<div>
  <Button variant="primary" onClick={this.add}>Add</Button>
  <Table striped bordered condensed hover>
    <thead>
    ...
```

Remember to import *Button* from 'react-bootstrap' :

```
import { Table, Button } from 'react-bootstrap';
```

When we click this button, we route to a new page with a form to add a new user. To create this route, implement the *add()* method in User.js as shown below.

```
add(e) {
    this.props.history.push("/add");
}
```

Remember that *this.props.history.push* navigates the user to the specified target route. Also remember to bind *add()* to our class in the constructor:

```
constructor(props){
    super(props);
    this.state = {
```

```
        users: []
    };
    this.add = this.add.bind(this);
  }
```

## App.js

In App.js, import and add the path to UserForm component as shown below. UserForm contains the form to add a user. We will create UserForm component in the next section.

```
import React, { Component } from 'react';
import User from './User';
import UserForm from './UserForm';
import {BrowserRouter, Route, Switch} from 'react-router-dom';

class App extends Component {

  render() {
    return (
      <div>
          <BrowserRouter>
          <div>
            <Switch>
              <Route path="/add" component={UserForm} />
              <Route exact path="/" component={User} />
              <Route path="/*" component={NotFound} />
            </Switch>
          </div>
        </BrowserRouter>
      </div>
    );
  }
}
...
```

## UserForm.js

Next, create the new component UserForm.js that implements a form with fields, *username* and *email* as shown below. Note that the UserForm code is rather lengthy and you can copy it from my GitHub repo at https://github.com/greglim81/react-chapter9. Also remember to run *npm install formik --save* to install *formik*.

```
import React, { Component } from 'react';
import { Formik, Form, Field, ErrorMessage } from 'formik';
import * as firebase from 'firebase';
```

112

```
class UserForm extends Component {

  render(){
    return(
      <div>
          <h1>{this.title}</h1>
          <Formik
            initialValues={{ username: '', email: '' }}
            validate={values => {
              let errors = {};
              if (!values.email) {
                errors.email = 'Required';
              } else if (
                !/^[A-Z0-9._%+-]+@[A-Z0-9.-]+\.[A-Z]{2,}$/i.test(values.email)
              ) {
                errors.email = 'Invalid email address';
              }
              else if (values.email.length < 10) {
                errors.email = 'Email address too short';
              }

              if (!values.username) {
                errors.username = 'Required';
              }
              else if (values.username.length < 3) {
                errors.username = 'username too short';
              }

              return errors;
            }}
            onSubmit={(values, { setSubmitting }) => {
              setTimeout(() => {
                // actual submit logic...
                firebase.database().ref('/').push({
                    username: values.username,
                    email: values.email
                }).then(() => this.props.history.push("/"));

                setSubmitting(false);
              }, 400);
            }}
          >
            {({ isSubmitting }) => (
              <Form>
```

```
          <Field type="email" name="email" />
          <span style={{ color:"red", fontWeight: "bold" }}>
            <ErrorMessage name="email" component="div" />
          </span>
          <Field type="text" name="username" />
          <span style={{ color:"red", fontWeight: "bold" }}>
            <ErrorMessage name="username" component="div" />
          </span>
          <button type="submit" disabled={isSubmitting}>
            Submit
          </button>
        </Form>
      )}
    </Formik>
  </div>
  )
 }
}

export default UserForm;
```

## Code Explanation

Although the above UserForm code is rather lengthy, much of the code should be familiar to you as explained in **Chapter 6: Forms**. If not, go back to that chapter for a revision.

*FirebaseListObservable Push*

Here I would like to focus on on*Submit()*which is called by the form upon submit.

```
onSubmit={(values, { setSubmitting }) => {
  setTimeout(() => {
    // actual submit logic...
    firebase.database().ref('/').push({
        username: values.username,
        email: values.email
    }).then(() => this.props.history.push("/"));

    setSubmitting(false);
  }, 400);
}}
```

To add an object to firebase, we use the *push* method from our *firebase.database().ref('/')* which we covered earlier in listing users. *push* generates and writes to a new child location with the value supplied. It writes

114

to the new child location using a unique key as covered previously when we stored this key in *user.key*. Unique keys are designed to be unguessable (they contain 72 random bits of entropy).

To be able to add an object to firebase, we need to have write permission. Earlier on, we have set this to *true* in the firebase console.

When the operation to add a new user completes, we are notified because we have subscribed to it using *then*. We then navigate back to the list of users with *this.props.history.push("/")*.

*Running your app*

Run your app now. Go to the **Add** form, enter in a new username and email and upon submitting the form, you should be able to see your new user object added to the list.

## 9.6 Deleting a User

Next, we want to delete a user by clicking on the delete icon in a row of the user list following which, a delete dialog box will appear asking us if we want to delete the user (fig. 9.6.1).

figure 9.6.1

*User.js*

To implement this, we first add two properties, *showDeleteDialog* and *selectedUser* to our component state:

```
class User extends Component {

  constructor(props){
    super(props);
    this.state = {
        users: [],
        showDeleteDialog: false,
```

```
    selectedUser: {}
  };
}
```

*showDeleteDialog* is used to decide when to show a delete dialog. When *showDeleteDialog* is false, we don't show the delete dialog. We set it to true when the delete button is clicked to show the delete dialog. *selectedUser* holds the current selected user so that we know which specific user to delete.

Next, we bind the on*Click* event of the delete button to the *openDeleteDialog()* method with *user* object (from firebase) as argument.

```
render() {
  const listUsers = this.state.users.map((user) =>
  <tr key={user.key}>
    <td>{user.username}</td>
    <td>{user.email}</td>
    <td>Edit</td>
   <td>
     <Button
     onClick={ this.openDeleteDialog.bind(this,user) }>Remove</Button>
    </td>
  </tr>
  );
```

Next, we implement the *openDeleteDialog()* method:

```
openDeleteDialog(user){
  this.setState({
      showDeleteDialog: true,
      selectedUser: user
  });
}
```

*openDeleteDialog* simply sets *showDeleteDialog* to true to show the delete dialog which we will implement in *render()* later. It also sets *selectedUser* to the user which is clicked.

## Delete Dialog

For the delete dialog, we make use of the *Modal* component (fig. 9.6.2) from react-bootstrap (https://react-bootstrap.github.io/components.html#modals).

figure 9.6.2

In react bootstrap site, 'Overlays', 'Modals', copy the markup for 'Static Markup' and paste into *render()* as shown in **bold** below:

```
import { Table, Button, Modal } from 'react-bootstrap';

...

    return (
      <div>
        <Button variant="primary" onClick={this.add}>Add</Button>
        <Table striped bordered condensed hover>
        <thead>
          <tr>
            <th>Username</th>
            <th>Email</th>
            <th>Edit</th>
            <th>Delete</th>
          </tr>
        </thead>
        <tbody>
          {listUsers}
        </tbody>
        </Table>
        <Modal show={this.state.showDeleteDialog} onHide={this.closeDeleteDialog}>
          <Modal.Header closeButton>
            <Modal.Title>Delete User</Modal.Title>
          </Modal.Header>
          <Modal.Body>
            <p>Are you sure you want to delete
                {this.state.selectedUser.username}?</p>
            <hr />
          </Modal.Body>
          <Modal.Footer>
            <Button onClick={this.delete}>Delete</Button>
            <Button onClick={this.closeDeleteDialog}>Close</Button>
          </Modal.Footer>
        </Modal>
      </div>
    );
```

117

## Code Explanation

```
<Modal show={this.state.showDeleteDialog} onHide={this.closeDeleteDialog}>
```

First, we set the *show* attribute of *Modal* to *this.state.showDeleteDialog*. The Modal will only show when *this.state.showDeleteDialog* is true.

We next bind *closeDeleteDialog* to the *onHide* event which is called when the Modal is hidden. We will implement *closeDeleteDialog* later which simply sets *showDeleteDialog* to false and *selectedUser* to null.

```
<Modal.Header closeButton>
  <Modal.Title>Delete User</Modal.Title>
</Modal.Header>
<Modal.Body>
 <p>Are you sure you want to delete
        {this.state.selectedUser.username}?</p>
  <hr />
</Modal.Body>
```

We then specify the descriptions we want to appear in the header and in the body as shown in the above code. We customize the prompt message with `{this.state.selectedUser.username}` to show the user name that we are about to delete.

```
<Modal.Footer>
  <Button onClick={this.delete}>Delete</Button>
  <Button onClick={this.closeDeleteDialog}>Close</Button>
</Modal.Footer>
```

In Modal Footer, we bind *delete()* to the *Delete* button and *closeDeleteDialog* to the *Close* button.

*closeDeleteDialog() and delete()*

```
closeDeleteDialog() {
  this.setState({
      showDeleteDialog: false,
      selectedUser: {}
  });
}
```

*closeDeleteDialog* sets the state's *showDeleteDialog* to false to hide the delete Modal and also sets *selectedUser* to null.

```
delete(e) {
  firebase.database().ref('/'+this.state.selectedUser.key).remove()
```

```
    .then( x=> {
        console.log("SUCCESS");
        this.closeDeleteDialog();
    })
    .catch( error => {
        alert("Could not delete the user.");
        console.log("ERROR", error)
    });
}
```

In the *delete()* method, we reference the specific user node location to delete in firebase database with *firebase.database().ref('/'+this.state.selectedUser.key)*. The location of the user node is contained in the *key* property of the user we have clicked to delete. Remember that we have the *key* property because whenever we add an object to firebase, a unique key is generated for us. We use this unique key stored in *key* to retrieve the object for deletion and later update.

After getting the user object, we then call its *remove()* method which returns a promise. We provide a callback which calls *closeDeleteDialog()* upon successful deletion. Any errors met while deleting can be caught in the *catch* callback. If successful, we log "Success", and if an error is caught, we log an error message.

Lastly, remember to bind the *closeDeleteDialog* and *delete* method with the below code in bold:

```
constructor(props){
    super(props);
    this.state = {
        users: [],
        showDeleteDialog: false,
        selectedUser: {}
    };
    this.add = this.add.bind(this);
    this.closeDeleteDialog = this.closeDeleteDialog.bind(this);
    this.delete = this.delete.bind(this);
}
```

## 9.7 Populating the Form on Edit

Having implemented, list, add and delete, we will now implement edit. Before we can implement edit, we need to retrieve the existing requested user object and populate it on the form first. When a user clicks on the **Edit** icon, she would be navigated to the User Form with the given user details populated in the input fields. We should also change the title of the page to **Edit User** instead of **Add User**. And if we access the User Form via the Add User button, title should be **New User**.

First in App.js, we define a new route *edit/:id* with *id* being a parameter as shown below. *id* will contain our user object id used to retrieve our *user* object and populate the Edit form. Remember that more specific route paths like '/edit/:id' should be specified first and other more inclusive paths like '/*' should be specified later.

*App.js*

```
<BrowserRouter>
  <div>
    <Switch>
      <Route path="/edit/:id" component={UserForm} />
      <Route path="/add" component={UserForm} />
      <Route exact path="/" component={User} />
      <Route path="/*" component={NotFound} />
    </Switch>
  </div>
</BrowserRouter>
```

*User.js*

Next, in User.js, we add the router link to the **Edit** icon with the parameter *user.key* used to retrieve our *user* object and populate our form.

```
const listUsers = this.state.users.map((user) =>
<tr key={user.key}>
  <td>{user.username}</td>
  <td>{user.email}</td>
  <td>
      <Link to={`/edit/${user.key}`}>
          Edit
      </Link>
  </td>
  <td><Button
onClick={ this.openDeleteDialog.bind(this,user) }>Remove</Button></td>

</tr>
);
```

Remember to import *Link* from *'react-router-dom'* in your import statements:

```
import React, { Component } from 'react';
import * as firebase from 'firebase';
import { Table, Button, Modal } from 'react-bootstrap';
import { Link } from 'react-router-dom';
```

*UserForm.js*

Next in UserForm.js, add the codes below in **bold**.

```
class UserForm extends Component {
  title;
  id;

  constructor(props){
    super(props);
    this.id = this.props.match.params.id;
    this.title = 'New User';
    this.state = {
      username: '',
      email:'',
    };

    if(this.id){
      this.title = 'Edit User';
    }
  }

  ...
```

Implement also the *componentDidMount* method as shown below:

```
  componentDidMount(){
    if(this.id){
        firebase.database().ref('/' + this.id)
        .on('value',snapshot => {
           this.setState({
               username: snapshot.val().username,
               email: snapshot.val().email,
           });
         });
    }
  }
```

Next, make the following changes in the Formik code:

```
          ...
        <Formik
          enableReinitialize={true}
          initialValues={{
```

```
    username: this.state.username,
    email: this.state.email
}}
...
```

*Code Explanation*

We retrieve *id* from *props.match.params.id*. In *componentDidMount*, we check if *id* is null, which means that we arrive at UserForm without a parameter and want to perform adding a new user. In this case, we use the default title of "New User" and do nothing in *componentDidMount*.

If *id* is valid (not null), it means that we arrive at UserForm with a parameter and want to perform editing an existing user. In this case, we set the title to "Edit User". We then proceed to retrieve the user object in *componentDidMount* with the below code:

```
componentDidMount(){
  if(this.id){
      firebase.database().ref('/' + this.id)
      .on('value',snapshot => {
          this.setState({
              username: snapshot.val().username,
              email: snapshot.val().email,
          });
        });
    }
}
```

We retrieving our *user* object by providing *id* as argument to *firebase.database().ref('/' + this.id)*. We subscribe to it and when we retrieve the snapshot, we set component state for *username* and *email* to the snapshot values. With *component state* now containing our requested user object, the form populates the *username* and *email* fields.

```
        ...
    <Formik
      enableReinitialize={true}
      initialValues={{
          username: this.state.username,
          email: this.state.email
      }}
      ...
```

We then render our Formik form with initial values of username and email retrieved from the database. We need to set *enableReinitialize={true}* so that the form reinitializes when *initialValues* prop changes, i.e. we get our username and email populated from the firebase callback function.

*Running your App*

If you run your app now, when you click on an existing user, you will be brought to the edit form which displays the title 'Edit User' with *username* and *email* fields populated (fig. 9.7.1).

## 9.8 Updating a User

Finally, to update the user, we make some code changes and additions to *onSubmit()* in UserForm.js. Fill in the below code into *onSubmit()*:

*UserForm.js*

...

```
            onSubmit={(values, { setSubmitting }) => {
              setTimeout(() => {
                // actual submit logic...
                if(this.id){
                    firebase.database().ref('/'+this.id).update({
                        username: values.username,
                        email: values.email
                    }).then(() => this.props.history.push("/"));
                }
                else{
                    firebase.database().ref('/').push({
                        username: values.username,
                        email: values.email
                    }).then(() => this.props.history.push("/"));
                }

                setSubmitting(false);
              }, 400);
            }}
```

...

*Code Explanation*

Similar to what we did in the population of the UserForm, we first check if there is an *id*, which means the form is in edit mode. If so, we call the *update* method of *firebase.database().ref* to *update*. Else, which means the form is in Add New User mode, we use the existing code which calls *push()* to add the new user object to firebase.

*Running your App*

If you run your app now, your app should have full functionality to create, update, delete and read user data from and to firebase.

## Summary

In this chapter, we learned how to implement C.R.U.D. operations using Firebase as our backend. We learned how to add firebase to our application, how to work with the firebase database from the firebase console, how to display a list of users, how to add a user with the push method, how to delete a user with the remove method, retrieve a single firebase object to prepare our form for edit and how to update a user.

With this knowledge, you can move on and build more complicated enterprise level fully functional React applications of your own!

Please feel free to email me at support@i-ducate.com if you encounter any errors with your code. Visit my GitHub repository at https://github.com/greglim81 if you have not already to have the full source code for this book.

# CHAPTER 10: INTRODUCTION TO REDUX

## 10.1 What is Redux?

Redux is a library that helps us manage the state of our application. It is typically used in medium to large applications with complex data flow. A simple application with simple data flow won't really need Redux. In fact, using Redux can add unnecessary complexity to our application. But what is considered a large application?

In a typical React app, each component maintains its own local component state. This fits well with the principle of encapsulation. But it can be a problem when there are multiple views that communicates with the same data especially when the views do not share a parent-child relationship.

In such scenarios, we often have multiple copies of the same data that are independent of one another. So, when a view updates the data, we need to do extra work to keep the other views' data in sync.

For example, in Facebook we have three views to represent the current state of user messages. First, we have the navigation bar icon (fig. 10.1.1) which shows the number of new messages.

Figure 10.1.1

Secondly, we have the new messages shown in the messages page and thirdly, we might have one or more chat tabs opened.

These are independent views that need to be in sync and they don't share a parent child relationship. For example, the navigator bar is not in a parent child relationship with the other views. If it was, we could use props to pass data down and back up.

To keep data in-sync in this case, we have to do extra work. A common solution is to use events. But when the app grows, it will turn into event spaghetti where we have events all over our code. To track what happens to the application state, we have to jump all over our code to find out. What makes our problem worse is that data is updated in an unpredictable manner. We have to track all over our code to figure out how data is flowing and how the application state is updated from multiple views. Also, adding a new feature would be a challenge because you don't know the impact of the new feature on the application state.

Facebook had this problem before in 2014 and they introduced the Flux architecture in response to it. Redux is a simplified, lightweight and elegant implementation of the Flux architecture so that we can manage our application state in a predictable way.

*Benefits*

Redux provides us with other benefits as well. Although Redux is often linked to React for management of application state in React applications, it's a standalone library. This means that state management is decoupled from the presentation framework e.g. React that we choose to use. We can use Redux with other presentation works like Angular, Vue or any other framework.

It also makes it easier for unit testing our application because Redux is heavily based on functional programming. For example, in the below code, we can unit test our adding and remove function that take in an existing state and returns a new state.

```
function reducer(state, action) {
    ...
    if (action.type === "ADD") {
        const newPerson = {
            id: action.personData.id,
            name: action.personData.name,
            age: action.personData.age
        }
        return {
            ...state,
            persons: state.persons.concat(newPerson)
        }
    } else if (action.type === "REMOVE") {
        return {
            ...state,
            persons: state.persons.filter(person => person.id !==
                                                action.personId)
        }
    } else {
        return state;
    }
}
```

Redux also makes it easier to implement undo and redo since all updates to state are captured. These benefits of course come at a cost. We have to add more code where there are more moving parts.

## 10.2 Transiting from Component States to Application State

As a general principle, you should start simple and use local component state first as introduced in this book. When your app grows, you can refactor components to use Redux to manage application state in a predictable way.

For example, in a Facebook application, you might have the following local component states initially:

```
App Component state:
loggedInUser: {
  name: "..."
}

Messages Component state:
messages: {
  {...},
  {...},
  {...}
}

  Message Component state:
  chatTabOpen: true

Posts Component state:
posts: {
  {...},
  {...},
  {...}
}

  Post Component state:
  expanded: false
```

Each component mutates its own state with internal *setState* calls. But as the app grows, it becomes difficult to determine the overall state of the application, where updates are coming from, which messenger tabs are open, which posts have been expanded etc. To find out, you have to traverse the component tree and track the state of these individual components.

Redux makes it easier for us to view our application state by having us store all state data in a single location called the Store. You can think of the store as a single JS object that acts as a local client-side database. From the single store, we manage the state of the current logged in user, messenger tabs open, posts etc. For example:

```
App state{
  loggedInUser: {
    name: "..."
  }

  messages: {
    {...},
    {...},
```

```
      {...}
    }
  chatTabOpen:  [3,6]

  posts: {
      {...},
      {...},
      {...}
  }
  postsExpanded:  [1]
}
```

Different views will then have different slices of the same store depending on their functionality. If one component makes changes to the store, changes are immediately visible to the other components. You don't have to search across multiple component states to find part of the state you want to update. Also, all data is ensured to be in-sync in a single store.

In the coming sections, we will introduce a simple Persons management application where we have person information stored in an array. A sample of our state will look like:

```
{
  persons:  [
      {id: 1, name:  "Greg", age:  5},
      {id: 2, name:  "Carol", age:  3},
      {id: 3, name:  "Gabriel", age:  6},
      {id: 4, name:  "Fred", age:  8}
  ]
}
```

Having identified our application's state structure, we will see how to change this state via actions.

## 10.3 Understanding the Redux Flow

In a React app, there are components which want to manipulate the app state. It doesn't do that by manipulating the central giant JavaScript store object. That would make our store unpredictable because if we can edit from anywhere in our application, we would not know where we made a certain change that broke our app for example. So, we need to have a clear and predictable process of updating the state. Redux is all about having a clearly defined process of how our state may change. We establish this predictable process by flowing data from actions, to our reducer, to the store and components subscribe to the store to receive state changes.

## Actions

The first building block of Redux are actions which are dispatched by components. Actions are simple data structures with no logic that describe what to change. They contain a *type* string property which describes the kind of action, something like 'Add Ingredient' or 'Remove Ingredient'.

Actions can also contain a 'payload' which contains the actual data for the performing of the actions. For example, if an action is of type 'Add Ingredient', the action payload will be the information for the ingredient to be added. If an action is of type 'Remove Ingredient', the action payload will be which ingredient to remove.

So, an action is simply an information package that we are sending to Redux. It doesn't directly change the store and doesn't hold any logic. It is merely a messenger of instructions about what should change in the application state along with the necessary data to make those changes. We should emphasize that in Redux, actions are the only way to update our state in Redux.

## Reducers

The thing that changes the store is the reducer. The reducer will check the type of the action and execute the logic for that kind of action and finally update parts of the state.

A reducer is just a pure function which receives the action and the existing state, and outputs a new updated state. Or in other words:

```
(state, action) => newState
```

We should emphasize that **the existing state is never modified or mutated**. Rather, the reducer always returns a new state which replaces the old state in the store. The logic in the reducer determines the final result of the updated new state.

## Store Subscriptions

Now that the central store is up to date, how do we communicate the updated state back to our component? We use a subscription model. The store triggers all subscriptions whenever the state changes. Our components can subscribe to the updates and receive them automatically. We will see a sample implementing of actions, reducers and store subscriptions in the next few sections.

# 10.4 Setting Up Reducer and Store

For now, we will build a simple console app that has no UI to illustrate how Redux works. Our app will allow you to add persons and remove persons. The purpose of the app is not to show UI-rich apps like those we have built in previous chapters, but to illustrate using simple code how Redux works. In the next chapter, we will illustrate using Redux with React UI.

For simplicity, we won't be using *create-react-app* to build a React project. We will simply work with a single HTML file that references the Redux library. We can later run the HTML file by opening it in our Chrome browser.

First, in VSCode (or your favourite code editor), create a new file called Persons.html and add in the following markup.

```html
<!DOCTYPE html>
<html>
  <head>
    <title>List of Persons</title>
    <script src="https://unpkg.com/redux@latest/dist/redux.js"></script>
  </head>
  <body>
    <script>
    </script>
  </body>
</html>
```

What we have now is just a basic HTML file which references a hosted version of the Redux library so that we can do away with the additional Redux installation steps for now. This also shows that Redux can work independent of React. In the next chapter, we will go through the actual installation steps for Redux to connect to React. But for now, we just reference the library directly.

## 10.5 Defining Actions

First, we define our actions. As mentioned, actions are the only way to communicate with our store. Inside the *script* tag, add the following shown in bold:

```html
<body>
  <script>
      function addPerson(id,name,age) {
          return {
              type: "ADD",
              personData: {
                  id: id,
                  name: name,
                  age: age
              }
          }
      }
```

```
function removePerson(id) {
    return {
        type: "REMOVE",
        personId: id
    }
}
</script>
</body>
```

Our two functions *addPerson* and *removePerson* each return an *action* object. Here, you see the *action* object consisting of a *type* property which describes what kind of action we are performing. In our case, we have two action types "ADD" and "REMOVE". It's up to you what description you want to give.

Other than *type*, we have what we call the 'payload' value of the action. In *addPerson*, our payload is

```
personData: {
    id: id,
    name: name,
    age: age
}
```

In *removePerson*, our payload is just:

```
personId: id
```

*addPerson* has a *personData* object which in turn contains several properties as its payload since we need these properties to describe the person we are adding. *removePerson* however only requires *id* as payload since we only need *id* to know which person to delete.

Both *addPerson* and *removePerson* have only one purpose which is to return an action. These functions are formally known in Redux as 'Action Creators' because they return *action* objects.

## 10.6 Reducer

Actions specify 'what' is to be done. 'How' it is done is left to the reducer. The reducer acts as an intermediary between the store and actions. To illustrate this, add the following reducer code below the action creator functions.

```
const initialState = {
    persons: []
};

function reducer(state, action) {
```

```
    if (state === undefined) {
        state = initialState;
    }
    if (action.type === "ADD") {
        const newPerson = {
            id: action.personData.id,
            name: action.personData.name,
            age: action.personData.age
        }
        return {
            ...state,
            persons: state.persons.concat(newPerson)
        }
    } else if (action.type === "REMOVE") {
        return {
            ...state,
            persons: state.persons.filter(person => person.id !==
                                          action.personId)
        }
    } else {
        return state;
    }
}
```

*Code Explanation*

```
const initialState = {
    persons: []
};

function reducer(state, action) {
    if (state === undefined) {
        state = initialState;
    }
```

Firstly, we initialize state to *initialState* (an empty *persons* array) if state is undefined to begin with. This happens for example, when we launch our app the first time. This ensures that we always have a state to work with.

The rest of the code is a series of if-else statements where we handle our actions. The reducer method gets the *action* object which gives the reducer access to the action *type* and *payload*.

Notice that each if-else clause caters to a particular action type and also returns a new state. Very important to note is that reducers should never alter its arguments, perform side effects like API calls, routing transitions or call non-pure functions like Date.now() or Math.random(). Reducers should be pure functions. That is, given the same arguments, it should always return the same next state with no argument mutation. It should be a pure function which always return the same result given the same arguments or in other words, be **predictable**.

```
if (action.type === "ADD") {
    const newPerson = {
        id: action.personData.id,
        name: action.personData.name,
        age: action.personData.age
    }
    return {
        ...state,
        persons: state.persons.concat(newPerson)
    }
}
```

In the "ADD" clause above, notice that we don't mutate the given *persons* array using *persons.push()*. This would mutate the existing state. Instead, we use '*...state*' to create a copy of the existing state and then replace the existing *persons* array in it. The *state.persons.concat* method returns a new array that contains the old values along with the added new person.

```
} else if (action.type === "REMOVE") {
    return {
        ...state,
        persons: state.persons.filter(person => person.id !==
                                            action.personId)
    }
}
```

When the action type is "REMOVE", we return a new array with the specified person removed using the *filter* method.

By now, you should understand that we shouldn't be modifying state but instead be returning a new one. Else, your Redux application will break.

```
} else {
    return state;
}
```

Lastly, if we get any other action type, we return our current state unaltered.

## 10.7 Connecting Actions, Reducer and Store

Next, we create our store and tie our reducer function to it by adding the below code to Persons.html:

```
var store = Redux.createStore(reducer);
```

We create a new store with *Redux.createStore* and provide our reducer as argument. With this, we have linked our actions, reducers and store together.

To see how it all works together, we call the dispatch method of the *store* object and provide it with an action as argument. Add the following codes:

```
store.dispatch(addPerson(1,"Greg",5));
store.dispatch(addPerson(2,"Carol",3));
store.dispatch(addPerson(3,"Gabriel",6));
store.dispatch(addPerson(4,"Fred",8));
store.dispatch(removePerson(4));
```

In the above code, each dispatch method sends the provided action to the reducer which then goes through its logic and return a new state.

To see the store's state each time the application state is modified, add the following:

```
var store = Redux.createStore(reducer);
store.subscribe(showState);

function showState () {
    console.log(store.getState());
}
```

*store.getState* returns the state's value. We then enclose this into a showState function which we provide as argument to *store.subscribe*. Stores allow us to subscribe handler functions that will be called each time the store completes dispatching an action. This will log the state's value into the developer console each time *dispatch* is called to fire an action (fig. 10.7.1).

```
▼ {persons: Array(1)}
  ▶ persons: [{…}]
  ▶ __proto__: Object
▼ {persons: Array(2)}
  ▶ persons: (2) [{…}, {…}]
  ▶ __proto__: Object
▼ {persons: Array(3)}
  ▶ persons: (3) [{…}, {…}, {…}]
  ▶ __proto__: Object
▼ {persons: Array(4)}
  ▼ persons: Array(4)
    ▶ 0: {id: 1, name: "Greg", age: 5}
    ▶ 1: {id: 2, name: "Carol", age: 3}
    ▶ 2: {id: 3, name: "Gabriel", age: 6}
    ▶ 3: {id: 4, name: "Fred", age: 8}
      length: 4
    ▶ __proto__: Array(0)
  ▶ __proto__: Object
▼ {persons: Array(3)}
  ▼ persons: Array(3)
    ▶ 0: {id: 1, name: "Greg", age: 5}
    ▶ 1: {id: 2, name: "Carol", age: 3}
    ▶ 2: {id: 3, name: "Gabriel", age: 6}
      length: 3
    ▶ __proto__: Array(0)
  ▶ __proto__: Object
```

Figure 10.7.1

In the above log, we can see our state after each *dispatch*. Particularly in the fifth state, we see that "Fred" has been removed after *removePerson(4)* has been dispatched.

In the next chapter, we will see how to connect React and Redux and provide a real-world example.

# CHAPTER 11: REACT WITH REDUX

In the last chapter, we learned about Redux and how to use it to manage an application's state data. In this chapter, we are going to combine React UI with the Redux store. We will be creating a simple cart app which users can add/remove products. The app will calculate the total cost of all the products and also provide 'Remove' links for user to remove a product from the cart (fig. 11.0.1).

| Learn Ionic | 17 | Add Product |

| Product Name | Product Price | # |
| --- | --- | --- |
| Learn React | 19 | Remove |
| Learn Angular | 19 | Remove |
| Learn Ionic | 17 | Remove |

Total Amount: 55

Figure 11.0.1

First, we use *create-react-app* to create our app called *reduxcart*:

```
create-react-app reduxcart
```

Next, navigate to the *reduxcart* directory and install Redux and *react-redux* dependencies with the following command:

```
npm install redux
```

```
npm install react-redux
```

*react-redux* is a framework used to integrate a Redux store with React components. It provides us with the Provider component that we use to set up our store as we will see soon.

## 11.1 Building our App

We will start with a clean project so that we do not have unnecessary files to clutter our learning. Go to the *src* and *public* folders and delete all the files in those folders. Then, in *public* folder, create a new file index.html with the following HTML:

*index.html*

```
<!doctype html>
<html lang="en">
  <head>
    <title>Redux Cart</title>
  </head>
  <body>
    <div id="container">
    </div>
  </body>
</html>
```

Next, in *src* folder create a new file index.js with the following codes:

*index.js*

```
import React, { Component } from "react";
import ReactDOM from "react-dom";
import { createStore } from "redux";
import { Provider } from "react-redux";
import cartReducer from "./reducer";
import App from "./App";
import 'bootstrap/dist/css/bootstrap.css';

var destination = document.querySelector("#container");

var store = createStore(cartReducer);

ReactDOM.render(
  <Provider store={store}>
    <App />
  </Provider>,
  destination
);
```

*Code Explanation*

```
var store = createStore(cartReducer);
```

First, we create our store with the *createStore* method that takes in our reducer *cartReducer* as argument. We have imported *cartReducer* in the above import statements and will be implementing that later.

```
<Provider store={store}>
  <App />
</Provider>
```

We then pass in our store to the Provider component as a prop. The Provider component has to be the enveloping outermost component to ensure that every component has access to the Redux store.

*reducer.js*

Next in the *src* folder, create a file reducer.js with the following code:

```
// Reducer
// Reducer
function cartReducer(state, action) {
    if (state === undefined) {
      return {
        totalCost: 0,
        productCart: []
      };
    }

    switch (action.type) {
      case "addProduct":
        return {
            ...state,
            totalCost: state.totalCost+parseInt(action.productData.productPrice),
            productCart: state.productCart.concat({
                productName: action.productData.productName,
                productPrice: action.productData.productPrice
            })
        }
      case "deleteProduct":
        const updatedArray = state.productCart.filter(product =>
                product.productName !== action.productData.productName);
        return{
            ...state,
            totalCost: state.totalCost-parseInt(action.productData.productPrice),
            productCart: updatedArray
        }
      default:
        return state;
    }
  }

export default cartReducer;
```

139

*Code Explanation*

```
function cartReducer(state, action) {
    if (state === undefined) {
      return {
        totalCost: 0,
        productCart: []
      };
    }
}
```

First, we initialize our state to an empty *productCart* array and *totalCost* being zero.

```
    switch (action.type) {
      case "addProduct":
        return {
            ...state,
            totalCost: state.totalCost+parseInt(action.productData.productPrice),
            productCart: state.productCart.concat({
                productName: action.productData.productName,
                productPrice: action.productData.productPrice
            })
        }
      case "deleteProduct":
        const updatedArray = state.productCart.filter(product =>
                product.productName !== action.productData.productName);
        return{
            ...state,
            totalCost: state.totalCost-parseInt(action.productData.productPrice),
            productCart: updatedArray
        }
      default:
        return state;
    }
```

We use a *switch* statement to handle the two action types (*addProduct* and *deleteProduct*) our reducer will receive. If the action type is *addProduct*, we increment *totalCost* by the product price and return a new array with the newly added product. If the action type is *removeProduct*, we subtract product price from *totalCost* and return a new array with the target product omitted.

Note that when we increment or decrement from *totalCost*, we have to use the *parseInt* method to convert string to numeric. Else, you will get a string with the numbers concatenated instead of added/subtracted.

140

## App.js

In *src* folder, create a new file App.js with the following code:

```
import { connect } from "react-redux";
import Cart from "./Cart";

function mapStateToProps(state) {
  return {
    totalCost: state.totalCost,
    productCart: state.productCart
  }
}

function mapDispatchToProps(dispatch) {
  return {
    onAddProduct: (productName, productPrice) => dispatch({
        type: "addProduct",
        productData: {
            productName: productName,
            productPrice: productPrice
        }}),
    onDeleteProduct: (productData) => dispatch({
        type: "deleteProduct",
        productData: productData
    })
  }
}

var connectedComponent = connect(
  mapStateToProps,
  mapDispatchToProps
)(Cart);

export default connectedComponent;
```

## Code Explanation

There are two main functions here, *mapStateToProps* and *mapDispatchToProps*. As their names suggest, they connect to Redux and provide these connections as props to our component.

```
function mapStateToProps(state) {
  return {
    totalCost: state.totalCost,
    productCart: state.productCart
  }
}
```

*mapStateToProps* subscribes to store updates and returns an object that contains a slice of the store data that we wish to make available as props to our component. In our case, we are making available *totalCost* and *productCart*.

```
function mapDispatchToProps(dispatch) {
  return {
    onAddProduct: (productName, productPrice) => dispatch({
        type: "addProduct",
        productData: {
            productName: productName,
            productPrice: productPrice
        }}),
    onDeleteProduct: (productData) => dispatch({
        type: "deleteProduct",
        productData: productData
    })
  }
}
```

*mapDispatchToProps* provides our component with access to the action creator functions that can be called to dispatch an action to the store. The *onAddProduct* function dispatches an action with action type "addProduct" and *productData* object as payload. The *onDeleteProduct* function similarly dispatches an action with action type "deleteProduct" and *productData* as payload. Both actions will be handled by the reducer we have created earlier on.

```
var connectedComponent = connect(
  mapStateToProps,
  mapDispatchToProps
)(Cart);
```

We then connect *mapStateToProps* and *mapDispatchToProps* to our Cart component so that it has access to *totalCost*, *onAddProduct* and *onDeleteProduct* as props. This is done using the *connect* method shown above.

The *connect* method returns a new higher order *Cart* component connected to the Redux store. The

142

higher order Cart component has added access to actions and dispatch calls that connects to the Redux store. You can think of it similar to extending an existing class. *connect* takes in *mapStateToProps* and *mapDispatchToProps* function as arguments and passes them to the extended Cart component. This is how a slice of the store and action creators are made available to components in general. React handles these automatically.

## Cart.js

Now, we create our Cart component. In *src* folder, create a new file Cart.js with the following code.

```
import React, { Component } from "react";
import AddProduct from './AddProduct';
import { Table } from 'reactstrap';

class Cart extends Component {
 render() {
   return (
     <div className="container">
        <AddProduct addProduct={this.props.onAddProduct}/>
        <Table>
           <thead>
           <tr>
              <th>Product Name</th>
              <th>Product Price</th>
              <th>#</th>
           </tr>
           </thead>
           <tbody>
              {this.props.productCart.map(productData => (
                 <tr key={productData.productName}>
                    <td>{productData.productName}</td>
                    <td>{productData.productPrice}</td>
                    <td onClick={() =>
                 this.props.onDeleteProduct(productData)}>Remove</td>
                    </tr>
              ))}
           </tbody>
        </Table>
      <span>Total Amount: {this.props.totalCost}</span>
     </div>
   );
```

```
    }
};
```

```
export default Cart;
```

*Reactstrap CSS*

To style our table, we use the Table component from the *reactstrap* library (http://reactstrap.github.io/). Install *reactstrap* and peer dependencies via NPM with the following command:

```
npm install --save reactstrap react react-dom
```

Reactstrap does not include Bootstrap CSS so this needs to be installed as well:

```
npm install --save bootstrap
```

*Props*

The cart consists of a simple AddProduct form and a table which lists the added products. We use the props sent from the connect HOC we implemented earlier. *this.props.onAddProduct*, *this.props.onDeleteProduct(productData)* functions are called when the add button and remove buttons are clicked respectively. Note that *this.props.onAddProduct* is passed as a prop *addProduct* to AddProduct component. This allows the AddProduct child component to dispatch actions to update application state directly instead of passing data back up the tree. We will be looking at it later. Also, *this.props.totalCost* is used to display the total cost.

```
<tbody>
    {this.props.productCart.map(productData => (
        <tr key={productData.productName}>
            <td>{productData.productName}</td>
            <td>{productData.productPrice}</td>
            <td onClick={() =>
                this.props.onDeleteProduct(productData)}>Remove</td>
        </tr>
    ))}
</tbody>
```

We use the Table component from *reactstrap* to create a nice-looking table. To populate table rows, we use the map function to populate each row with product name and price. We also provide a 'remove' column which calls *props.onDeleteProduct* which dispatches action of type *deleteProduct* to our reducer to remove that product from the cart array.

## *AddProduct Component*

Lastly, we create our AddProduct component (AddProduct.js) with the following code:

```
import React, { Component } from "react";

class AddProduct extends Component {

    state = {
        productName: '',
        productPrice: 0
    }

    productNameChangedHandler = (event) =>{
        this.setState({productName: event.target.value});
    }

    productPriceChangedHandler = (event) =>{
        this.setState({productPrice: event.target.value});
    }

    render() {
        return (
            <div className="container">
                <input
                    type="text"
                    placeholder="Product Name"
                    onChange={this.productNameChangedHandler}
                    value={this.state.productName}
                />
                <input
                    type="number"
                    placeholder="Product Price"
                    onChange={this.productPriceChangedHandler}
                    value={this.state.productPrice}
                />
                <button className="buttons"
                    onClick={() => {

this.props.addProduct(this.state.productName,this.state.productPrice);
                    }}>Add Product</button>
```

```
        </div>
    );
  }
};
```

```
export default AddProduct;
```

Our AddProduct component is a simple form. If the form code seems unfamiliar to you, refer back to chapter six for a refresher on how React forms work. Note that in *AddProduct*, we have both local component state *productName* and *productPrice* which are used to store the values entered into the input fields. So, you can have both local component states working in conjunction with application wide Redux state. Local component states are typically for use in the local component where other components do not require access.

Finally, in the *onClick* handler of the button, we have our *addProduct* prop which dispatches the *addProduct* action type to our reducer with the input values from product name and product price fields. As mentioned earlier, this is an example where we dispatch actions directly from child components to update application state.

*Running your app*

If you run your app now, you should see your Cart working as expected. In this chapter, we looked at how to connect Redux to React. We used react-redux to help us connect the Redux store to the React presentation to create a working app.

# CHAPTER 12: FUNCTION OR CLASS-BASED COMPONENTS? INTRODUCING HOOKS

The components we have so far gone through in this book are class-based components that support state and life-cycle methods. There is another kind of component called functional component that is defined by a function. E.g.

```
import React from 'react';

function App() {
  return(
    <div>
      <h1>
        My First React App!
      </h1>
    </div>
  );
}

export default App;
```

So, should we use a functional-based component or class-based one?

Firstly, both are still React components. That is, a component can either be implemented with a function, or with a class. Regardless of its implementation, the purpose of a component is to ultimately produce HTML to the user (via JSX). Its secondary purpose is to handle feedback from the user, e.g. user clicks, typing of the keyboard.

One of the challenging things to do when first introduced to React is to decide if she should use a class-based or functional-based component. It is here that I wish to give you a general rule of thumb to one just beginning React. Functional-based components are good for showing simple content to the user without a lot of logic behind it. That is, you have some amount of JSX and you can return it without much complicated processing.

Now, a class-based component is used generally if you have complex logic e.g. you need to respond to user input, make network requests etc.

I personally enjoy working with class-based components but there are many professional developers out there who would disagree with me. The community around React is quite split on this topic. Some will say, I will try to use as many functional components as I can, others will say, use class-based components.

147

The advantages that class-based components give us include: they can access component level 'state', making it easier to handle input and update its view with *setState*. Class-based components also provide lifecycle events e.g. *componentDidMount*, *componentDidUpdate* thus making it easier to do some tasks when the app first starts up.

Now what about functional-based components? They return JSX but don't really have state, lifecycle methods and thus don't have much logic associated with them. But React Hooks is going to change all that.

With Hooks, functional-based components can now have component level state and life cycle methods. But is Hooks just about functional components replicating functionality from class-based ones? If it were so, why not just continue using class-based components?

What we are going to see in the following sections is that Hooks is going to make it easier to **share** logic between different components which can be hard to address using class-based components. Hooks in essence allow us to re-use logic.

*App Overview*

To illustrate the usage of hooks, we will work on a new project. Create a new project called hello_hooks with:

```
create-react-app hello_hooks
```

Our simple project will fetch data from https://jsonplaceholder.typicode.com/, a fake online REST API for testing and prototyping (fig. 12.1).

## Resources

JSONPlaceholder comes with a set of 6 common resources:

| | |
|---|---|
| /posts | 100 posts |
| /comments | 500 comments |
| /albums | 100 albums |
| /photos | 5000 photos |
| /todos | 200 todos |
| /users | 10 users |

Figure 12.1

Our app will have two button links to retrieve posts and todos (fig. 12.2).

148

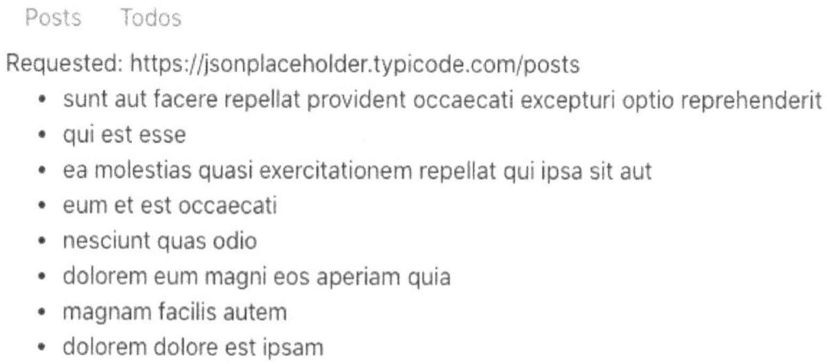

Posts    Todos

Requested: https://jsonplaceholder.typicode.com/posts

- sunt aut facere repellat provident occaecati excepturi optio reprehenderit
- qui est esse
- ea molestias quasi exercitationem repellat qui ipsa sit aut
- eum et est occaecati
- nesciunt quas odio
- dolorem eum magni eos aperiam quia
- magnam facilis autem
- dolorem dolore est ipsam

Figure 12.2

Because we will be using react-bootstrap, run:

```
npm install react-bootstrap bootstrap
```

*Class-based Component*

In App.js, suppose we have the below simple class-based component.

```
import React from 'react';
import 'bootstrap/dist/css/bootstrap.min.css';
import { Button } from 'react-bootstrap';

class App extends React.Component{
  state = { requested: '' };

  render(){
    return(
      <div>
        <Button variant="link" onClick={() => this.setState({
          requested: 'https://jsonplaceholder.typicode.com/posts'
          })}>
          Posts
        </Button>
        <Button variant="link" onClick={() => this.setState({
          requested: 'https://jsonplaceholder.typicode.com/todos'
        })}>
          Todos
        </Button>
```

149

```
        <br />
        Requested: {this.state.requested}
      </div>
    )
  }
}

export default App;
```

Our component shows two buttons with each setting *requested* in state to either a *posts* url or *todos* url. *requested* thus shows what resource we are currently requesting.

## Reconverting a Class to a Function

Now, we will make use of hooks to refactor this to a functional component with a state.

Before we refactor, let's first have a quick introduction to the different functions the hook system provides. The hook library provides the following functions:

*useState* – allows a functional component to use component level state
*useEffect* – allows a functional component to use life cycle methods
*useContext* – allows a functional component to use context system.
*useRef* – allows a functional component to use *Ref* to make reference to a DOM element

In this chapter, we will cover on *useState* and *useEffect*.

To converting our class compoment to a functional component, in App.js, change it to the following:

```
import React, { useState } from 'react';
import 'bootstrap/dist/css/bootstrap.min.css';
import { Button } from 'react-bootstrap';

const App = () => {

  const postsUrl = "https://jsonplaceholder.typicode.com/posts"
  const todosUrl = "https://jsonplaceholder.typicode.com/todos"
  const [requested, setRequested] = useState(postsUrl)

  return(
    <div>
      <Button variant="link" onClick={() => setRequested(postsUrl)}>
```

```
        Posts
      </Button>
      <Button variant="link" onClick={() => setRequested(todosUrl)}>
        Todos
      </Button>
      <br />
      Requested: { requested }
    </div>
  )
}
```

```
export default App;
```

*Code Explanation*

```
import React, { useState } from 'react';
```

Firstly, we import *useState* from the react library as we will be using it for hooks. The rest of the import statements remain the same as the class component.

```
const App = () => {
```

We then have the declaration of the function *App*.

```
  const [requested, setRequested] = useState(postsUrl)
```

The above is a crucial line where most of our explanation will go into. As mentioned, the *useState* provides state to a functional component. The above line is saying that we have a variable *requested* in our state, and we set its initial value to *postsUrl*. This line is the same as *state = { requested: postsUrl }* in our class component.

And *setRequested* is the setter method to update the value of this piece of state. That is, *setRequested(postsUrl)* is the same as *this.setState({requested: postsUrl })}* in the class component.

This is shown in the Button's *onClick*, where you have:

```
      <Button variant="link" onClick={() => setRequested(postsUrl)}>
        Posts
      </Button>
```

which is the same as:

```
<Button variant="link" onClick={() => this.setState({requested:postsUrl})}>
  Posts
</Button>
```

in the class component.

Technically, in:

```
const [requested, setRequested] = useState(postsUrl)
```

*useState* returns two elements. The first element returned is assigned to *requested* which contains the current value of this piece of state. The second element returned is assigned to *setRequested* which is the setter to update this piece of state.

So previously in our class component, our state is an object with values in it. i.e.

```
state = { requested: postsUrl };
```

But with the *useState* hook, we declare a value in our state one at a time i.e.

```
const [requested, setRequested] = useState(postsUrl)
```

In hooks, we move away from declaring an object containing all of our state to declaring the individual state variables themselves. For example, suppose we want a counter in our state. In a class component, it would be:

```
state = {
  requested: postsUrl,
  count: 0
};
```

But for states in a functional component, it would look like:

```
const App = () => {
  const [requested, setRequested] = useState(postsUrl)
  const [counter, setCounter] = useState(0)
```

...

And just as *setState* re-renders a class component each time it is called; in functional components, each time a setter, i.e. *setRequested* or *setCounter* is called, the functional component will be re-rendered.

## Data Fetching with *useEffect*

In class components, we would typically do data fetching in *componentDidMount*. We illustrated that in chapter nine where we requested for users' data.

Now, how do we achieve the same effect for *componentDidMount* in functional components? That's where *useEffect* comes in. *useEffect* serves the same prupose as *componentDidMount*, *componentDidUpdate* and *componentWillUnmount* in functional components but unified as a single function.

Thus, we put the request data logic into *useEffect* as shown:

```
import React, { useState, useEffect } from 'react';
...
const App = () => {

  const postsUrl = "https://jsonplaceholder.typicode.com/posts"
  const todosUrl = "https://jsonplaceholder.typicode.com/todos"

  const [requested, setRequested] = useState(postsUrl)
  const [data, setData] = useState([])

  useEffect(() =>{
    fetch(requested)
      .then(response => response.json())
      .then(data => setData(data))
  },[])

  return(
      ...
  )
}
export default App;
```

*Code Explanation*

```
import React, { useState, useEffect } from 'react';
```

We first import *useEffect* from the react library.

```
  const [data, setData] = useState([])
```

We also declare an array *data* that holds the requested data in our state. We initialize *data* to an empty array `[]`.

```
  useEffect(() =>{
    fetch(requested)
      .then(response => response.json())
      .then(data => setData(data))
  },[])
```

And we call *useEffect* like the above. Note that instead of calling *this.setState({data: data})*, we use *setData(data)*.

Now, why is there an empty array fed into the second argument of *useEffect?* Remember that *useEffect* serves the same purpose as *componentDidMount*, *componentDidUpdate* and *componentWillUnmount*. But how do we differentiate the use of *useEffect* between the three?

*Infinite useEffect*

If we implement *useEffect* without specifying the 2nd parameter, i.e.:

```
  useEffect(() =>{
    fetch(requested)
      .then(response => response.json())
      .then(data => setData(data))
  })
```

It is then equivalent to *componentDidUpdate.*, which runs every time the component gets new props, or a state change happens.

That is, if you run the app now, and you go to your 'Network' tab under the Chrome Developer Tools, you can see that the request to *posts* is being sent repeatedly in an infinite loop (fig. 12.3)!

| Name | Status | Type | Initiator | Size | Time | Wa |
|------|--------|------|-----------|------|------|-----|
| posts | 200 | fetch | App.js:10 | 69 B | 12 ms | |
| posts | 200 | fetch | App.js:10 | 69 B | 11 ms | |
| posts | 200 | fetch | App.js:10 | 69 B | 19 ms | |
| posts | 200 | fetch | App.js:10 | 69 B | 14 ms | |
| posts | 200 | fetch | App.js:10 | 69 B | 10 ms | |
| posts | 200 | fetch | App.js:10 | 69 B | 11 ms | |
| posts | 200 | fetch | App.js:10 | 69 B | 15 ms | |
| posts | 200 | fetch | App.js:10 | 69 B | 12 ms | |
| posts | 200 | fetch | App.js:10 | 68 B | 23 ms | |
| posts | 200 | fetch | App.js:10 | 69 B | 11 ms | |
| posts | 200 | fetch | App.js:10 | 69 B | 12 ms | |
| posts | 200 | fetch | App.js:10 | 69 B | 12 ms | |
| posts | 200 | fetch | App.js:10 | 69 B | 12 ms | |
| posts | 200 | fetch | App.js:10 | 69 B | 11 ms | |
| posts | 200 | fetch | App.js:10 | 464 B | 16 ms | |
| posts | 200 | fetch | App.js:10 | 69 B | 11 ms | |
| posts | 200 | fetch | App.js:10 | 69 B | 12 ms | |
| posts | (pen... | fetch | App.js:10 | 0 B | Pen... | |

Figure 12.3

This is because *useEffect* does the request and then updates the state with *setData*, which thus calls *useEffect* again!

Thus, to mimic *componentDidMount*, we have to pass in an empty array as a second argument to *useEffect* where the request will be made only once.

```
useEffect(() =>{
  fetch(requested)
    .then(response => response.json())
    .then(data => setData(data))
}, [])
```

*Displaying our Requested Data*

To render our requested data, add in the below map function:

```
return(
  <div>
    <Button variant="link" onClick={() => setRequested(postsUrl)}>
      Posts
    </Button>
    <Button variant="link" onClick={() => setRequested(usersUrl)}>
      Todos
    </Button>
    <br />
    Requested: { requested }
    <ul>
      {data.map(el =>(
        <li key={el.id}>{el.title}</li>
      ))}
    </ul>
  </div>
)
```

And when we run our app, the lists of requested post titles should appear (fig. 12.4):

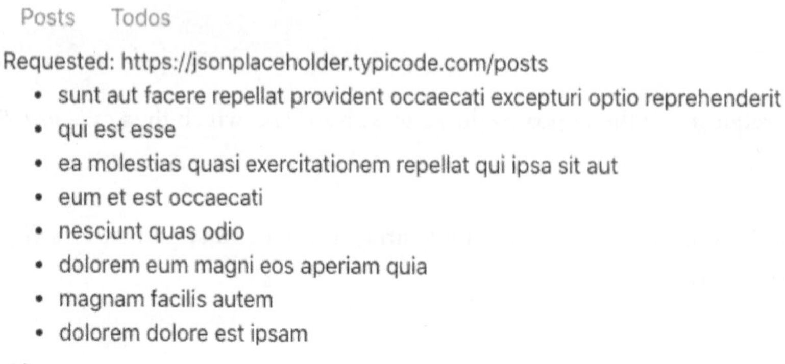

Posts    Todos

Requested: https://jsonplaceholder.typicode.com/posts
- sunt aut facere repellat provident occaecati excepturi optio reprehenderit
- qui est esse
- ea molestias quasi exercitationem repellat qui ipsa sit aut
- eum et est occaecati
- nesciunt quas odio
- dolorem eum magni eos aperiam quia
- magnam facilis autem
- dolorem dolore est ipsam

Figure 12.4

*Another Problem*

We now meet with another problem however, when we click on 'Todos', it should list out the todos also, but it doesn't! Why is that? That is because *useEffect* is called only once because we have configured it to be just like *componentDidMount*. When we click on the 'Todos', *useEffect* does not get called again just as *componentDidMount*. What we want to achieve now is that whenever the value of *requested* in *useEffect* changes (i.e. from *postsUrl* to *todosUrl*), we want to call *useEffect* again. But if the *requested* doesn't change, don't do anything.

To achieve that, we simply specify the *requested* into the array:

```
useEffect(() =>{
  fetch(requested)
    .then(response => response.json())
    .then(data => setData(data))
},[ requested ])
```

And now, whenever *requested* changes in value, *useEffect* will be called. So, if you run your app now, when you click on *Todos*, it will be able to request *todos* as well.

Do note that *todos* can display without any problems because it also has the *id* and *title* attribute.

```
<ul>
  {data.map(el =>(
    <li key={el.id}>{el.title}</li>
  ))}
</ul>
```

## Extractable Reusable Logic

Now, we come to the section that makes React hooks really useful. We can encapsulate our logic in a React hook and then import that hook when we want to use it. For example, we will encapsulate our request logic in a hook. First, create a new file *useFetch.js*. Note that the filename containing a hook starts with a lower case. This is the general convention for hooks. Whereas for filenames containing components, it starts with an upper case e.g. *App.js*.

So in *useFetch.js*, move our *useEffect* code there like the below:

*useFetch.js*

```
import { useState, useEffect } from 'react';

const useFetch = (url) => {
  const [data, setData] = useState([])

  useEffect(() =>{
    fetch(url)
      .then(response => response.json())
      .then(data => setData(data))
  },[url])

  return data
}

export default useFetch;
```

And to use our newly custom created *useFetch* hook in App.js, make the below code changes:

*App.js*

```
import React, {useState, useEffect} from 'react';
...
import useFetch from './useFetch'

const App = () => {

  const postsUrl = "https://jsonplaceholder.typicode.com/posts"
  const todosUrl = "https://jsonplaceholder.typicode.com/todos"

  const [requested, setRequested] = useState('posts')
  const [data, setData] = useState([])
  const data = useFetch(requested)

  useEffect(() =>{
    fetch(requested)
      .then(response => response.json())
      .then(data => setData(data))
  },[requested])
```

```
   return(
       ...
   )
}

export default App;
```

Just the above few lines of code changes are needed. And the output remains the same. This is what make hooks so attractive. We can encapsulate logic into their own functions that other components can re-use. It makes it easier to reuse logic between components. Also, our code in App.js is cleaner and leaner.

This might not seem as a big improvement, but it actually is because *useFetch* has no tie to any specific component. We can reuse *useFetch* in any other component. For e.g. if we want to request users from *https://jsonplaceholder.typicode.com/users*, we can just pass in that route and get back the response from that end point.

Let's illustrate this by fetching users and print out their name with our newly created *useFetch* hook. Create a new file Users.js with the following code:

```
import React from 'react'
import useFetch from './useFetch'

const Users = () => {
    const users = useFetch("https://jsonplaceholder.typicode.com/users")

    return(
      <ul>
        {users.map(el =>(//
          <li key={el.id}>{el.name}></li>
        ))}
      </ul>
    )
}

export default Users
```

And then in App.js, we render the *Users* component with:

```
...
import Users from './Users'

const App = () => {

    ...
  return(
    <div>
      <Users />
      <Button variant="link" onClick={() => setRequested(postsUrl)}>
        Posts
      </Button>
....
```

By re-using the *useFetch* hook, we didn't have to write a single link of code around making a request inside of the *Users* component. We just have:

```
const users = useFetch("https://jsonplaceholder.typicode.com/users")
```

We didn't have to re-code any network request logic. So, this is an example of how to construct hooks and re-use logic between components.

## Summary

With this knowledge, you can move on and build more complicated enterprise-level fully functional React applications of your own!

Hopefully, you have enjoyed this book and would like to learn more from me. I would love to get your feedback, learning what you liked and didn't for us to improve.

Please feel free to email me at support@i-ducate.com if you encounter any errors with your code or to get updated versions of this book. Visit my GitHub repository at https://github.com/greglim81 if you have not already have the full source code for this book.

This book has largely focused on React development through class components. I have written a separate book ("Beginning React with Hooks", *https://www.amazon.com/dp/B088ZT9P36/*) which brings you through React development using function components.

If you have bought this book but also want to get up to speed with React development using Hooks, just drop me a mail at support@i-ducate.com and I will give you a complimentary copy of "Beginning React with Hooks" as a way to expressing my thanks to you for purchasing this book.

Thank you and all the best for your learning journey in React!

## About the Author

Greg Lim is a technologist and author of several programming books. Greg has many years in teaching programming in tertiary institutions and he places special emphasis on learning by doing.

Contact Greg at support@i-ducate.com.

Lightning Source UK Ltd.
Milton Keynes UK
UKHW030626280921
391315UK00009B/534